Praise for

CARRY YOUR HEART

"'What can I do today to honour those who have travelled on?' Answering this question through his extensive practice as a nīhithaw psychotherapist, Louis Busch shows how personal pain, when steered by Elders' insight, helps us face life's challenges through curiosity, flexibility, and wide-open hearts."

John Borrows (Chippewas of the Nawash First Nation), OC, FRSC, Loveland Chair in Indigenous Law, Henry N.R. Jackman Faculty of Law, University of Toronto, and author of *The Seven Cycles of Life*

"A beautifully written book that skilfully blends ancient wisdom with modern science. Profound, poetic, and pragmatic. Step-by-step, with great compassion, Louis Busch will guide you through facing your fears, transcending your suffering, becoming the sort of person you truly want to be, and living your life to the fullest. Highly recommended!"

Dr. Russ Harris, bestselling author of *The Happiness Trap*

"In this empathic and inspiring book, Louis Busch shares his transformative vision for navigating personal crisis, grief, and loss through creative and insightful integration of his own Indigenous Cree values with the science of psychological flexibility. Specifically, Louis interrelates three traditional teachings—belonging through kinship, presence in the world, and purposeful action—with the principles of acceptance and commitment therapy to promote healing and pursue well-being. With great sensitivity and compassion, he encourages us all to learn to 'move through our lives with emotional and spiritual openness, awareness and intention'—in short, to walk while carrying our hearts."

Joseph P. Gone (Aaniiih-Gros Ventre), PhD,
professor of anthropology and of global health
and social medicine, Harvard University

"Louis Busch takes your hand for a journey down a pathway of Indigenous knowledge, understanding, and renewal. . . . Busch is fulfilling two prophecies: first, to know more about oneself and how to stand in that gifted place, and second, that Indigenous ways are created by generosity of the heart for sharing and healing. I, for one, hold his hand in gratitude for bringing me with him on this sacred way of life."

Dr. Dolores Subia BigFoot (Caddo Nation of Oklahoma),
PhD, child psychologist and former director
of the Indian Country Child Trauma Center
at the University of Oklahoma Health Sciences Center

CARRY YOUR HEART

Indigenous Helping Wisdom and the Science of Psychological Flexibility

LOUIS BUSCH, PhD

INTRODUCTION BY STEVEN C. HAYES, PhD

PUBLISHED BY SIMON & SCHUSTER

New York Amsterdam/Antwerp London
Toronto Sydney/Melbourne New Delhi

SIMON & SCHUSTER
CANADA

A Division of Simon & Schuster, LLC
166 King Street East, Suite 300
Toronto, Ontario M5A 1J3

The authorized representative in the EEA is Simon & Schuster Nederland B.V., Herculesplein 96, 3584 AA Utrecht, Netherlands. info@simonandschuster.nl

This Simon & Schuster Canada edition September 2026

Interior design by Wendy Blum

Interior illustrations copyright © Hotdog Water Art, Tsista Kennedy

Manufactured in the United States of America

10 9 8 7 6 5 4 3 2 1

Online Computer Library Centre number: 1564285441

ISBN 978-1-6682-0617-1
ISBN 978-1-6682-0619-5 (ebook)

For Jerome

CONTENTS

A NOTE ON LANGUAGE

The teachings, stories, and words shared in this book come from relationships with Elders, Knowledge Keepers, family, and community across particular nations, places, and contexts. Because of this, readers will notice variations in spelling, pronunciation, translation, and usage. In some cases, I have retained dialectal and locally preferred forms in order to honour the original speakers and translators, as well as the knowledge shared in those settings.

I am deeply grateful to Simon Bird for his generous guidance with Cree language throughout the manuscript, and to Gloria Oshkabewisens-McGregor for her guidance and corrections regarding the Anishinaabemowin used in this book. Their care and knowledge greatly strengthened this work.

That said, any errors, limitations, or misunderstandings that remain are mine and mine alone.

Louis Busch

FOREWORD
LEARNING WITH AN OPEN HEART

One of the most humbling lessons of psychological science is that human suffering and human flourishing are both universal and profoundly particular. Every culture, every family, every person wrestles with the question of how to live a good life, but the answers are never identical. They are shaped by land, language, Ceremony, history, and the lived realities of communities.

Louis Busch's *Carry Your Heart* stands in this space between the universal and the particular. It is a book rooted in Cree, Anishinaabe, and other Indigenous teachings, and it is also in dialogue with the science of psychological flexibility.

Reading these pages, I was reminded that science does not own wisdom. At its best, it is a knowledge development strategy that needs to learn to listen, to be guided, to consider, and to serve.

LISTENING BEFORE SPEAKING

So much of scientific psychology has been shaped by the impulse to explain, to diagnose, to categorize. This book turns us towards a different posture: to listen, to receive, to let meaning unfold in relationship. Louis recalls visiting with Grandmother Renée Thomas-Hill, who described the heart, body, mind, and spirit as members of a family—each with a role to play, each with wisdom to share. The heart as Grandmother, the body as Mother, the spirit as Great-Grandmother, and the mind as the impulsive Child who must learn to listen. That image says more about the relational nature of well-being than any manualized treatment protocol ever could.

To listen to such teachings is not to do so with a goal of translating them quickly into psychology as if the wisdom of Indigenous Peoples should line up and be inspected, categorized, and declared to be "discovered." I think listening means first to honour wisdom on its own terms, while noticing the resonances within yourself. Psychological flexibility, for example, does indeed suggest that our minds can race ahead of us, insisting on control, and that healing comes when we soften, attend, and reconnect with what matters. But the teaching of the family of heart, body, mind, and spirit does not need science to validate it. It stands as a gift in its own right.

PAIN AS TEACHER, NOT ENEMY

Another thread woven throughout this book is the recognition of pain as part of life, even as a teacher. Coast Salish educator Len Pierre describes emotions as nutrients to be digested. Grief, anger, fear—they may all feel unbearable at times, yet they carry signals that orient us towards love, healthy boundaries, or needs for rest. If we resist emotions, they fester, and their messages to us become muddled. If we let them pass through so they can fulfill their function, they can nourish us and guide us.

This teaching aligns with one of the central insights of acceptance and commitment therapy (ACT): that our attempts to eliminate or control pain often amplify it, while learning how to be more willing to feel can open us to life. Yet again, the Indigenous framing adds layers of wisdom. Emotions are not only private events inside the skin—they are relational, cultural, spiritual. They link us to ancestors and descendants, to land and language. That perspective expands what psychological flexibility means. It is not only about coping with inner states, but about walking rightly in an ongoing web of relations.

GRIEF, CONNECTION, AND SHARED HUMANITY

Louis writes with heartbreaking honesty about the loss of his brother. He names grief as a visitor that does not follow neat stages but comes in waves, sometimes with guilt, sometimes with silence, sometimes with laughter. In Ceremony, he hears Elders describe grief as a responsibility—to carry forward the memory of those who have gone, to let their lives continue through ours.

This reframing of grief—as kinship, as continuity—expands and enriches how I understand psychological flexibility. In ACT, we say pain is inevitable, but suffering is shaped by how we relate to it. In *Carry Your Heart*, grief is not a problem to be solved at all. It is an obligation of love, a bond that does not end with death. That is not suffering; it is a face of belonging.

LANGUAGE AND WORLDVIEW

Again and again, this book reminds us that language carries worldview. Where English says, "I am depressed," Cree may say, "Her heart is turning its face away." Where English makes *self* a noun—a thing, an object—Indigenous languages often render experience and sense of self as a verb, as relationship. These linguistic shifts are not cosmetic. They invite different possibilities for living.

A runaway horse, a tree bending in the wind, seaweed wrapping around the legs of a frightened swimmer, metaphors such as these reach the heart far more quickly than technical terms. Contextual behavioural science has long embraced metaphor and story, and it is learning to embrace image, movement, and song. It is good to have multiple language systems. This beautiful book reminds us that all our technical frameworks are only one way of speaking among many.

A MEETING OF WORLDS

The most dangerous form of cultural connection is appropriation—pasting the work of others on a therapy manual and calling it "cultural." Louis is careful to avoid what he calls pasting feathers and beads on an existing treatment manual. He allows Indigenous helping knowledges to speak first and then places them in a dialogue with psychological science. The result is not a dilution of either, but a synergy of perspectives that can guide real human lives.

This humility is exactly what psychology itself needs. Too often, psychological science has treated culture as an afterthought, a variable to control. Yet science is itself a cultural activity, rooted in certain histories and values; even the very measures and analyses it applies are heavily culturally burdened, and increasingly, we realize, by some of the ugliest and most racist features of Western culture. I will not unpack that in this moment—rather I want to emphasize that by meeting Indigenous wisdom with respect, we all can learn that psychological processes are not abstractions detached from land and history. They are lived in families, in ceremonies, in grief, in laughter.

TOWARDS THE GOOD LIFE

Across traditions, people have asked, What does it mean to live a good life? Louis recounts the Cree teaching of kita-pimōtātamān kitēh—"I walk while carrying my heart." To live well is not to hide our hearts away, nor to set them down as too heavy. It is to carry them openly, with all the joy and sorrow, and to walk in balance with self, family, community, land, and spirit.

Psychological flexibility offers a parallel answer: to open up, be present, and move towards what matters. But reading this book, I am reminded once again that these processes are not new. They are not discoveries. They are faces of ancient teachings, carried in language, in Ceremony, in story. What the science can offer is not a replacement, but a complementary lens. And what Indigenous knowledge offers science is a depth of context and relationship that science too often lacks.

WALKING TOGETHER

The pages that follow invite us into dialogue, not dogma. They ask us to approach with humility, curiosity, and respect. They remind us that difference is not a barrier but a gift. The journeys of Indigenous peoples—marked by both profound suffering and extraordinary resilience—are not to be compared with anyone else's. They are to be listened to, honoured, and learned from.

I have been privileged to spend many hours with Louis over the years. I can call him my friend. I have been honoured by conversations he structured with Indigenous Knowledge Keepers. I can literally hear his voice in these pages. Although your relationship with Louis is likely different, I suspect you will hear him as well.

His words speak. And as I listened to them I found my own understanding of my life and my life's work on psychological flexibility stretched and enriched. I saw more clearly that our struggles with pain are not only personal, but cultural and historical. I heard the message that pain is love in different form in a new way. I saw how values are not simply individual preferences, but kinship responsibilities. I saw how presence is not only awareness of inner states, but alignment with land, language, and spirit.

For readers who come from psychology, this book is an invitation to listen beyond the boundaries of our field. For readers who come from Indigenous communities, it is an affirmation of the wisdom you and your community carry. For all of us, it is a reminder that to live a good life is to carry our hearts—together.

Steven C. Hayes, PhD
Foundation Professor Emeritus of Psychology,
University of Nevada, Reno
President, Institute of Better Health
Originator of Acceptance and Commitment Therapy
Honoured Friend of Louis Paul Alexander Busch

CARRY YOUR HEART

PREPARING FOR THE JOURNEY AHEAD

I have fond memories of joining my mom, aunties, and grannies on excursions into the bush to pick berries and check the rabbit snares. It always felt like an adventure. I can't remember if I was given this task or whether it was self-appointed, but one of my jobs on these adventures was to spot the markers that had been left behind to signal the location of the snares. Usually, they were pieces of bright cloth or ribbon, a rock pile, or even a strategically placed bottle or can. I loved looking out the window of the truck or scanning the shoreline from some old boat while peeling my eyes for these wayfinders. I always felt so proud to spot one and point it out to my granny. I remember her big smile like I had just climbed Mount Everest, even though I now know that she most certainly knew where to go without any markers at all.

I've come to realize that in all the gestures and stories and seemingly ordinary activities, deep teachings were embedded for me about how to live in balance as part of the world. Those tattered cloth flags and sun-bleached cans were more than a game for a little boy; they led the way to sustenance and survival, they kept hands warm and bellies full in the North's frozen winters. In this way, the many strong women in my life have taught me to leave signs of care so I would not lose my way. Helpers do this. They mark what has been learned, where and from whom they learned it, and then they return often to see how the teachings have changed them. And when a gift is found that fills or heals, we bring it back to our families and nations.

That is the subtle teaching that nōhkom slipped under my ribs while I peeked through spruce bows on those adventures: pay attention, travel with a good heart, and leave something small and true so that the next to come can find their footing. This book is me tying what I can to low branches. It is not the whole path, only bright threads from my own journey that might catch your eye when the light hits them just right.

A journey begins with a question. What does it mean to carry your heart? This teaching was given to me by my Sun Dance brother, Ken Bighetty. Ken is a painter, a puppeteer, a leader, and a gifted helper from Pukatawagan, Manitoba. Anyone who has met Ken will tell you that he carries a warmth and energy that fills every space he enters. His smile and his laughter lift you up, even when you are deep within your suffering. He has a rare gift of moving between sincerity and humour with ease, and he is deeply committed to his family and community.

In one of our visits, Ken shared a teaching in nīhithawīwin, the Woodland Cree dialect: kita-pimōtātamān kitēh, which he explained means something close to "walk while carrying your heart," although English translations never do our words or concepts justice. It is a teaching about how we might move through our lives with emotional and spiritual openness, awareness, and intention rather than the detachment and automation that modern society seems to favour more and more these days. While we come into this world with a heart wide open, somewhere along the way, we set it down, hide it away, and stack heavy stones around it to keep it safe. To carry your heart means pushing those stones aside, picking your heart up, and walking with what you've lived through: your joy, sorrows, fears, hopes, and grief. It means walking in a way that honours and acknowledges your inner life, your relationships, and your place within the world around you. Each person may have a different understanding of these words and teachings. And that is okay. That is how it is supposed to be. But from what I've heard, I believe that learning to carry your heart is one way we begin to walk in the direction of a life of purpose and vitality, one that we might look back and smile at in our ripe old age.

So how do we do it? How do we carry our hearts when they can get so heavy? How do we move with intention when everything seems pitted against us? How do we return to the kind of openness and curiosity that we had when we arrived on this planet, before we were shaped and hardened by our pain and the pain of others? How do we rid ourselves of anxiety, fear, anger, and grief? How do we forgive? How do we learn to trust? To love? How do we live well?

If you've come to this book seeking a definitive answer to any of these questions, I am afraid you will be sorely disappointed. I do not currently have, nor do I anticipate ever possessing, such answers. But don't worry; I do not intend to send you home empty-handed after our visit. I hope that you will continue on your journey with some new supplies that will be of use on and off your path. Whether you are seeking personal healing, working to become a stronger helper, or hoping to contribute to the health of your community or nation, I hope that you will find something of value here. Whatever the reason, I am grateful that you have chosen to read these words.

Before we begin, there are protocols to follow. By picking up this book, you and I have entered into a relationship that I hope to honour in the best way I can from the distant time and place from which I am writing and you are reading. To do so, you are going to need to know some things about me, about where I come from, how I got here, and why I am writing this book. The name that I carry is wāwātewimistatim (ᐚᐚᐦᑌᐏ ᒥᐢᑕᑎᒼ), which translates to Northern Lights Horse in the Woodlands Cree dialect. I am a Bear Clan member of Nisichawayasihk Cree Nation. My helpers are the Loon, the Eagle, the Horse, and the Chickadee. My colours are white and the colours of the northern lights. My mother is Pauline Busch (née Spence) from piponapiwinihk (South Indian Lake), daughter of the late Louis and Verna Bonner. My father is Lennard Busch, a member of Kahkewistahaw First Nation and the son of John and Amy Busch. My maternal great-grandparents are Matilda and Frank Linklater. Matilda's mother, my maternal great-great-grandmother, was called Supila. I am a father, a partner, a helper, and a learner. By positioning myself in this way, I respectfully acknowledge the ancestors and the lands that have nurtured my family for generations. I also acknowledge the roles and responsibilities that I have to my family and community, and I lay the foundation for a relationship with you that is based on respect and reciprocity.

I am also a behavioural scientist and a registered psychotherapist working primarily with First Nations Peoples on the territories now referred to as Canada. For more than two decades I have done my best to walk with people on their healing journeys. I spent the first part of my career conducting assessments and designing treatment plans on locked inpatient units at a large psychiatric hospital, helping our relatives with neurodevelopmental differences whose severe aggression and self-injury threatened their health and safety. Next, I spent the better part of a decade supporting the healing journeys of men and women who had been found "not criminally responsible" for serious offences and who were subsequently mandated to receive treatment within Ontario's forensic mental health system. Working within "complex mental illness," as it is often referred to, is challenging and rewarding work. I have learned that human beings can experience almost unthinkable suffering, and yet, we are also capable of exceptional change and healing, even in the grimmest of circumstances. Most importantly, I learned the value of relationship in helping work and in healing. After many years within these institutions, my helping path brought me back to community, to walking with my relatives, First Nations Peoples who are struggling with their experiences and with the ongoing harms of colonization and intergenerational trauma.

While I have collected the relevant degrees, licences, and certifications along the way, I come by my experience in mental health honestly. My grandmother attended Guy Hill residential school at Sturgeon Landing. My mother is a survivor of the provincial Indian Day School system. Countless members of my extended family lost their childhoods and lives in these institutions, which were designed to "kill the Indian in the child" and were often characterized by the most vicious forms of abuse and neglect. Sadly, our family's story is not unique; the harms of the residential school system (the last of which only closed its doors in 1996 in Canada) continue to ripple out across Turtle Island, touching each and every Indigenous family and community. The result of this system of forced assimilation and its modern counterparts in health care, education, and social services has been a disproportionate burden of chronic disease, socioeconomic distress, mental health struggles, substance use, suicide, and a widespread state of anomie among Indigenous Peoples. My own family and community have worked hard to heal while being pummelled by continuous crisis and loss. As you can imagine, and as many of you reading know all too well, healing can feel like paddling upstream against a strong current.

I experienced my own mental health crisis shortly after high school. After being rejected from every university in the province on account of my terrible grades, I moved to the big city in the hopes of finding work and adventure. I soon had two jobs: demolition and loading trucks by day and stacking milk crates at a grocery by night. The little time I had left, I spent partying. The first number of weeks out on my own were exciting, but I soon began to feel lonely and suspicious of those around me.

I pushed good friends away with unjustified anger and paranoia and became more and more isolated. I would barricade my door and blast music as loud as possible to quiet my thoughts, which of course made my roommates, neighbours, and landlord furious. I didn't care. I felt betrayed by the world and somehow justified in my rage. I was losing touch with reality and quickly beginning to hate the person I saw in the mirror each morning. I was having trouble sleeping. When I closed my eyes, I could see faces that morphed in and out of focus, and I could hear my name spoken loudly whenever I started to drift off. I was terrified. So rather than sleep, I walked the city's north end until the early hours of the morning most nights. Before long, I had completely ostracized my roommates, two good friends who were also just trying to find their way away from home for the first time and who got to be on the receiving end of my deteriorating mental health. I was drinking heavily, often by myself or with the wayward folks I would meet in parks or under bridges. As I slept less and less, I got more and more angry and paranoid. I think a part of me knew something was wrong. It was like I was sitting in a dark theatre, watching my life unfold on a horrible slow-motion silent film.

All of this would culminate in a standoff with the police on the side of a bridge one crisp fall night. I was exhausted, tired of the loneliness, the shame, the night voices, and the feeling that I could see too much, feel too much, hear too much, and yet still not know where to put any of it. My thoughts had grown tangled and chaotic. I didn't understand what was happening to me; I only knew that I didn't want to feel it anymore. So I sat on the rail, looking down at the jagged rocks below. I had planned on ending my life that night, but instead ended up having a slumber party on a cream-coloured psych ward, listening to the screams of the other unfortunate travellers who seemed to be on this dark road with me.

That night marked a turning point. Not because of any great clinical breakthrough, but because of a weird guy in flip-flops and a Hawaiian shirt who sat with me and somehow reached through the fog. As the years pass, my memory makes him look more and more like Jeffrey "the Dude" Lebowski, and I'm sad that I never learned or at least cannot remember his real name. He didn't do anything particularly brilliant in a clinical sense; I don't think he was a nurse or therapist. He just showed up in all his awkward, radiant presence and carried his heart in a way I wasn't used to. Somehow, that made space for me to hold mine more gently, just long enough to get my feet back on the ground.

I managed to survive that bit and a few weeks later made my way home and spent some time reorienting myself to myself. My troubles didn't end there of course, but going home was the start of a slow journey of recovery with many painful bumps along the way. Being around my family and friends, doing physical work outside under the sun, and playing music again grounded me in a way I didn't realize I needed. I picked up writing again too, something I had abandoned in the chaos (I still regret tossing a stack of notebooks into a dumpster during a particularly dark moment before things fell apart). Slowly, quietly, things began to shift. I could breathe again. The world didn't seem quite as sharp around the edges.

After a series of odd jobs in construction and demolition, I landed a good job driving a forklift at a warehouse with three of my older brothers. There was something steadying about that too; monotonous predictability, lifting, scanning, and stacking, and knowing who had your back. Those years didn't offer any dramatic breakthroughs either, but they did give me what I needed: time, consistency, connection, and a little bit of space to begin imagining a different kind of life.

A decade or so later, just as I thought things were finally coming together, disaster struck again. I had worked hard to build a life that felt stable, or stable enough to tell myself I had put the spectre of mental illness behind me. I went back to school, found purpose in helping work, and met the love of my life. We were starting a family, and I was slowly learning what it meant to be accountable to others, to be part of something bigger than myself. I had the makings of a meaningful career as a front-line mental health professional, and a growing (if fragile) sense that I was becoming the kind of man that I wanted to be. But as I've learned time and time again since then, healing doesn't happen in straight lines. It circles back, kicks open old doors, slams others shut, and almost always arrives unannounced and uninvited at the worst possible timing.

In the middle of all of that supposed stability, I had my first intense panic attack. Now, I have always considered myself an anxious person, and I've been gifted with various diagnostic labels like "generalized anxiety disorder," "adjustment disorder," and "attention deficit hyperactivity disorder" in strange naming ceremonies with psychiatrists and psychologists over the years, but this was different. In a flash, it felt like the life force was leaving my body. A surge of primal fear shot up my brainstem. My hands tingled, my mouth went desert dry, my chest and throat tightened. I was overcome with an intense urge to do something, anything, while simultaneously blinded by a thick tangle of mental chaos that prevented me from thinking clearly enough to actually act in any sensible way.

I survived what I thought for sure was some mild heart attack or neurological crisis, and proceeded to do what everyone who first experiences this kind of panic does next: I went to the doctor and then to specialist after specialist in search of a logical medical explanation. Of course, while I searched, the attacks didn't stop. They got more intense, more frequent, and more unpredictable. While driving in the car, talking on the phone, or sitting in a clinical meeting at work, I would feel first the tingle at the back of my neck and then the heaviness in my chest, followed by a change in consciousness similar to the moments before one passes out. Tunnel vision, fear, confusion. My response would typically be to stop doing whatever I was doing in that moment or, if I wasn't doing anything, to start moving around in the hopes of preventing some undefined disaster. I would drink water, fan my face, sit down, stand up, take a deep breath, hold my breath, look down, look up, stretch my legs, wiggle my toes. And most of all, I would try to find some way to escape whatever setting I was in. On one particularly ridiculous occasion, I had an intense episode while driving past a police car, which caused me to careen onto the shoulder directly in front of him. Not very smooth at all.

As time went on, my belief that this was some sort of neurovascular issue led to a series of safety behaviours, which included a hyper-focus on hydration and electrolytes, taking sedatives or beta blockers in an effort to reduce my heart rate (my heart rate was normal), wearing compression socks used by diabetics (I don't have diabetes) to prevent blood from pooling in my legs (blood wasn't pooling in my legs), eating a salty snack and drinking a ton of water, and even carrying a small portable fan around. My world shrank as my list of safety strategies grew. As my anti-panic suit of armour got thicker, it also got heavier. So I began to avoid many of the people and places that had previously been very important to me, and the one drink to wind down after work soon turned into four or five. Things were quickly becoming intolerable.

The medical examinations of course found nothing. Somehow, I was healthy as a horse; damn it. Working in mental health, I was painfully aware of the propensity of panic-disordered patients to frantically search for a physiological explanation for their experience and to reject the idea that these horrible physical sensations could possibly be psychosomatic. "Relax, it's all in your head" is an anxiety sufferer's least favourite phrase, by the way. But this couldn't be the case for me. I'm an educated mental health professional, after all. I should know better. Right? Apparently not.

It took more than a year before I started to consider the possibility that the attacks could be anything but neurological or cardiovascular in origin. As I began to grapple with the uncomfortable possibility of "mental disorder," I decided to set to work on myself in the most clinical and systematic of ways. I would wield the full power of the science of human behaviour to fix myself. I educated myself on everything about panic disorder (I must have read one hundred scientific studies on the subject). I worked to identify and reframe the distorted automatic thoughts that might be contributing to the attacks. I rigorously documented my panic in the hopes of identifying common contextual and temporal patterns. I engaged in frequent progressive muscle relaxation exercises. I tried to increase awareness of the bodily sensations associated with the onset of panic, and I engaged in as much exposure work as possible by doing more of the stuff that I thought brought on panic rather than less. Finally, I saw a therapist and my physician (a lot).

After several years of this, I was disappointed that things hadn't improved much. I was looking for a cure that would ensure that I would never have to feel the cold grip of panic ever again, but there it was, lurking inside me and around every corner. To be fair to myself and those who were trying to help, the attacks did begin to occur less randomly. I was grateful for not having to pull the car over on the highway or to sit down after walking into a building and feeling dizzy, but I still found myself regularly paralyzed by that dreadful sensation and had begun to spend a lot of time also being anxious about the anxiety itself. I worried about when I might panic next, I worried about the possible sources of the anxiety, I worried about how well I was hiding my anxiety from others, I worried about what would happen if I could not get rid of the anxiety before the next important event. So in addition to struggling with intermittent panic attacks, my generalized or "free floating" anxiety was getting much worse. I couldn't sit in a chair without having an intense urge to act, and if I didn't have something specific to do, some looming deadline, I couldn't be at ease. I found the quiet deeply distressing.

I didn't mind so much being anxious as long as there was a clear reason for it, but if I couldn't identify a source, I felt terrible. So I poured myself into more and more work, more and more projects and papers and research studies and classes and volunteer work and deadlines. I figured if I had to be anxious, it might as well be for a good reason. I thank my lucky stars often that Lisa—my partner and best friend, who also happens to be a psychotherapist—put up with my endless freak-outs with patience, understanding, and compassion; I honestly don't know that I could have been so gracious should the tables have been turned.

While I was absurdly productive during this period of my life, things were still not improving on the anxiety front. My schedule gave me a good reason to be anxious, but now I found I was anxious about the amount of time I was spending distracted and away from my family, about how this pace of work was impacting my health, and about the risk of disappointing the people I had made commitments to with my endless list of projects. And of course, all these things generated their own little armies of anxiety-provoking agents. It seemed that all my efforts to eliminate my anxiety had only helped it to spread and intensify. When they teach you about anxiety in therapist school, they don't mention how tiring it is, how embodied the experience is. Anxiety fatigue and the impact on the body is truly awful. I was utterly exhausted all the time, but I couldn't rest. It's clear to me now why anxiety and depression often go hand in hand.

Despite my efforts, the super-scientific, systematic clinical approach to killing my anxiety was not doing the trick. As a mental health clinician who had spent the last decade recommending a similar approach to others, this was a hard pill to swallow. Could nothing be done? Was I doomed to a life of eating pretzels, chugging electrolytes, popping benzos and beta blockers, and donning weird compression socks before meetings, gatherings, and presentations? Would I spend the rest of my days working to the point of complete exhaustion each night just to avoid the torture of my own idle hands and mind? I really hoped not.

Now, if you're hoping to hear the secret cure that I then discovered that freed me from all the unpleasant experiences that come with anxiety—the self-doubt, depression, exhaustion, relational strain, hopelessness, and irritability—I am afraid that you will once again be sorely disappointed. I unfortunately have not found the cure for mental disorder on my travels and am not by any stretch of the imagination "cured," I'm sorry to say. But I did say I wouldn't let you leave this visit empty-handed. Two things happened that I believe have drastically changed my life and my relationship with psychological distress. Perhaps they will be of some use to you.

First, I began to reconnect with my culture. As a child, I was proud of being nēhīthāwāk, but as I grew older, experiences with racism and the weight of intergenerational trauma led me to distance myself from my Indigenous identity. It wasn't until I became a father myself that I felt a renewed motivation to reconnect with my Indigeneity. This reconnection has been a crucial part of my healing process and has brought me closer to understanding myself and my place in the world. This gradual journey of cultural reconnection, which I'll describe in more detail later in this book, has played an important role in shaping my understanding of wellness. It's a journey that continues to this day, one with teachings that inform both my personal life and my approach to helping others.

The second thing that I believe has been an important part of my healing journey was my introduction to the science of psychological flexibility and a psychotherapy called acceptance and commitment therapy (pronounced "act" rather than "A-C-T"). I had heard about contextual behavioural science and ACT in my clinical work and even cofacilitated a few groups that used the approach with neurodiverse patients at the hospital early in my career, but

I was not terribly interested or impressed at first glance. I was the last person to buy into things like "mindfulness," "present-moment awareness," or the "conceptualized self." (What does that even mean, right?) I am a proper behavioural scientist, and I like to think of myself as a pragmatic, evidence-focused, no-nonsense kind of mental health clinician. The concepts seemed much too fluffy to be useful in my empirically driven world. I wanted to be able to measure change through direct observation and see it on a graph, to count the scores on a structured assessment, not through someone's self-report of how psychologically flexible they felt after mindfully listening to a raisin. Yuck!

So mostly I ignored ACT and continued working with the trusty psychological problem-solving tools that had served me well in my clinical work in neurodevelopmental disability and forensic mental health for over a decade. But of course, those trusty tools failed to produce results when I tried repeatedly to use them to "fix" myself. The challenge was too complex to be put into a linear equation, and when push came to shove on my own distress, when medical science failed to produce answers and behavioural science failed to produce results, I started grasping beyond the tools and graphs for more.

I had also begun to do more counselling work with forensic patients who were given psychiatric labels like major depression, psychosis not-otherwise-specified, or borderline personality disorder. Like me, the nature of their suffering was exceedingly complex. I didn't have the heart to tell them to track and challenge their cognitive errors on a checky-box sheet or take deep breaths and squeeze a stress ball. So as one part necessity and one part curiosity, I decided to give contextual behavioural science another chance. I stumbled upon Kelly G. Wilson's books *The Wisdom to*

Know the Difference and *Things Might Go Terribly, Horribly Wrong* and was hooked.

I attended Kelly's workshop when he came to town. He wasn't the kind of mental health expert I had grown accustomed to. He was a psychologist but was unapologetically vulnerable and unabashedly fallible. And honestly, he looks more like the guys I used to party with when I was in rock bands than a world-renowned psychologist. Further, he knew the pain of deep loss and complex grief, having lost a brother to suicide. His story shook me to my core.

Then I heard Dr. Steven Hayes's story of struggling with panic attacks as a young professor and felt like I had found another kindred spirit. So I started attending every workshop, webinar, and training bootcamp I could. I devoured all the books I could find on the subject. I sought out clinical supervision from experts in the science of psychological flexibility, and most importantly, I found a skilled therapist for myself and began to look at my own experiences differently (thank you, Dr. Lee Unger). Again, this was not an overnight process, but something closer to a decade of learning and practice and mistakes and doubts and setbacks and discoveries. In fact, the journey continues to this day.

In addition to ACT, I have become very interested in the science underlying ACT. The science of psychological flexibility, known officially as contextual behavioural science, is a field of research that focuses on understanding and improving human behaviour by first considering the context in which it occurs. In essence, contextual behavioural science is about using a scientific approach to understand human behaviour and applying that knowledge to help people lead better lives.

There is a very complex model of language and cognition that serves as the foundation for the science called relational frame theory or RFT, but I won't spend very much time on this, as many of the readings on relational frame theory are excellent treatments for insomnia (they'll put you to sleep quick!). I would, however, encourage you to seek out more information on these topics should you be interested in the "stuff under the hood," as Dr. Russ Harris lovingly calls it.

The important thing is that when I stopped holding my cultural identity and clinical training in separate hands and began to carry my whole heart, as it were, a new way of working and living took form. This integration reshaped how I understand suffering and how I try to move through the world. It has strengthened my practice as a helper and deepened my life as a father, partner, and human being. To be sure, neither of these perspectives have eliminated my pain, but they have taught me how to carry it. That's what this book is about. I've been on a long and winding road shaped by Ceremony, clinical science, and lived experience. My hope is that what I've seen and gathered along the way can be of some use to you as you carry your heart through this weird human journey of ours.

In the world of contextual behavioural science, a psychologically flexible stance is most simply described as one that is open, aware, and engaged. In this book, I work with these qualities through three nīhithaw teachings: otōtīmowin, ākāwāmisowin, and mithotōtamowin. I introduce each of these teachings in its own section later and use them to expand the psychological flexibility model from a Cree perspective on how to help, heal, and live well. In the chapters that follow, one eye is provided by the generous Elders and Knowledge Keepers who have shared their stories and teachings with me, and the other by my perspective as an Indigenous academic, clinician, and researcher on a long healing journey.

The psychological flexibility model evolved within Western psychology, but the principles it describes also live within Indigenous knowledge systems. We have held and shared these teachings for millennia. There are terms for these ideas found deep within our languages. We find them in rich supply in our stories and within our ceremonies. Really, cultures and spiritual traditions across the world have practised mindfulness and perspective taking, explored the self, and considered the relationship between mind, heart, and body since we became capable of doing so.

The science of psychological flexibility offers one useful way of approaching human suffering. As we explore the synergies and differences together, the ideas may feel familiar. You may already carry many of these teachings through your grandparents' stories, your morning prayers, your nation's healing ceremonies, or your own life experience. I think this is because the concepts speak to similar truths about the human journey. While meeting with Elders and Knowledge Keepers, Dr. Hayes acknowledged something he also reflects on in the foreword to this book: that the science of psychological flexibility is, in many ways, catching up to understandings long held within ancient wisdom traditions. I appreciated the humility and respect of that acknowledgement, especially coming from the founder of ACT.

* * *

When I started on my healing journey, I didn't imagine that the two worlds I was exploring would eventually collide. The science of psychological flexibility and Indigenous helping wisdom were both having a positive effect in my life, and I was convinced that there were interactions between the two that could be of practical use for the many relatives across Turtle Island who are struggling with the residue of several lifetimes of colonial trauma, with the self-doubt, shame, and self-hatred that comes with it.

I wanted to build something that I could also use in my work as a helper. But I wanted to do this in a meaningful way; I wanted it to be a true partnership of perspectives, a deep-level adaptation that reflects Indigenous values from the start. I have attended too many mental health training sessions touting the phrase *cultural adaptation* that look more like a regular ole Western therapy manual decorated with beads and feathers and a bald eagle soaring over the cover. I did not want to do that. How could I share what I had found in a meaningful and respectful way? How could I bring the two healing philosophies together without trivializing one or the other? This seemed like a daunting task.

Luckily, there are protocols for seeking knowledge on daunting tasks. I started by making an offering of cistīmāw (tobacco) to a number of Elders and Knowledge Keepers and was thrilled with the opportunity to learn from Renée Thomas-Hill, Len Pierre, Isaac Murdoch, Vivian Recollet, Gloria Oshkabewisens-McGregor, and Ron Linklater. Over a number of years, I have visited with each of them to ask questions, to listen, and to discuss how the two perspectives might complement each other. I've also had a hand from some brilliant clinicians along the way, including Steve Hayes, Benjamin Schoendorff, and Matthieu Villatte. Of particular note has been my psychological partner in crime Lesley Barreira. Lesley is a behaviour analyst who has an insatiable passion for learning and is always putting me onto new and exciting adventures in the mysteries of the human condition. Lesley is a masterclass in humility and will likely die by cringing while reading this, but she has been such an important part of this work, I can't help but gush about her a bit. Seeing the Elders and clinicians come together will be a memory I will cherish for many years to come. It was clear from what they shared with one another that there were indeed opportunities for cross-pollination of the two healing philosophies. After this, I knew I was on the right path.

As Indigenous Peoples, we find ourselves shaped by languages and stories passed down over generations, while also navigating the structures and expectations of modern settler society. It is often said that we walk two paths as we try to find balance across contexts that do not always align. Walking two paths can be challenging. Leroy Little Bear, a Blackfoot Elder and professor emeritus at the University of Lethbridge, spoke of "colliding worldviews" when describing the struggle of simultaneously holding a precolonized consciousness and a colonized consciousness, and suggested that we have an "integrated mind, a fluxing and ambidextrous consciousness." I think he's right.

In my psychotherapy practice, I often see cultural dissonance as a source of significant distress for the First Nations Peoples I walk with. When we integrate Indigenous helping wisdom and one or more Western psychological modalities, it can be risky and challenging, but may also offer some unique benefits. Ron Linklater, a gifted Knowledge Keeper and teacher, shared the Anishinaabemowin word *agwadaazowin*. He described it as having a relationship with Indigenous philosophies, worldviews, and ideas about our connection to Mother Earth, the Spirits, the Grandfathers and Grandmothers, and the Creator, while also being open to learning from the good qualities of other helping philosophies. He said to think of it as the same energy that is meant to go into the creation of sacred treaties. My hope in pulling these threads together is to offer something that might be of value by drawing on the strengths of Indigenous wellness philosophies and the science of psychological flexibility.

Before beginning this journey, it is important to say something about what I mean when I refer to "Indigenous wisdom." Immense diversity exists among Indigenous nations across North America and around the world. Each nation holds its own customs, social and political life, language, and spiritual practice. In this work, I have drawn on teachings shared with me by Elders and Knowledge Keepers from several nations, including nēhiyaw, Anishinaabe, Coast Salish, and Haudenosaunee communities. Even so, the perspectives included here cannot represent all Indigenous teachings, nor could any single book hope to do so. There is no single, unified Indigenous identity. While there are sometimes shared philosophical threads across nations, ideas such as relationality or interconnection, these are expressed in distinct ways within each community. Histories, practices, and ways of living differ widely, shaped by place, language, and lived experience. What is offered here reflects particular teachings shared in particular contexts, not a comprehensive account of Indigenous knowledge as a whole.

As a result of colonization, there are differences in the extent of cultural continuity present in each community. Some communities have deep connections to language and traditional teachings and practices, while others may practise strict adherence to one of many Christian denominations. Further, communities rarely have a uniform spiritual or religious perspective shared by all, as individuals and families within these communities may have their own distinct beliefs and practices. Recognizing and honouring these differences is crucial for fostering understanding, reciprocity, and cultural humility.

Throughout this book I use the term *Indigenous* to refer broadly to First Nations Peoples in Canada, but I also endeavour to minimize these generalizations and use the names of specific nations whenever possible. In doing so, my hope is to avoid the illusion of a pan-Indigenous approach to wellness or the possible existence of a singular Indigenous psychotherapy. In fact, it may very well be the case that "Indigenous psychotherapy" is an oxymoron, and that the complexity of Indigenous wellness practices cannot be captured by the common categorizations of the psy disciplines. The goal here is not to invent new practices or dilute existing traditions, but to explore how traditional teachings and modern psychological approaches might complement each other in ways that are beneficial for those who are suffering. The intention is to open a dialogue about how Indigenous helping wisdom and contemporary psychology might work together, while fully respecting the diversity, autonomy, and specificity of one another's perspective. Nēhiyaw scholar Willie Ermine from Sturgeon Lake Cree Nation refers to this as the *ethical space of engagement*.

This balance is important. Indigenous lives are often pathologized by the modern mental health system, which is built on Euro-Western values and an assumption of universal applicability. Diagnostic labels and symptom language tend to locate problems inside the individual, treating suffering as a matter of disordered biology, personality, or cognition. In doing so, much is left out. The realities of colonial and neocolonial power. The material conditions shaped by poverty and dispossession. The cumulative weight of racism, institutional harm, environmental exposure, and chronically underfunded social systems. These contexts are not background noise. They are often central to the distress itself. This kind of individualization shifts responsibility away from the systems that produce harm and onto the people who live with its consequences. If something is wrong inside of me, then it becomes my fault and my task alone to manage or repair. But what if this framework is part of the problem rather than the solution? What if our efforts to suppress, control, or normalize difficult experiences are contributing to suffering rather than easing it? Is there another way? I hope to explore this possibility with you in the pages that follow.

Finally, certain teachings and practices are not meant to be shared within the pages of a book. Sacred knowledge and healing are best found in Ceremony and in relationship with an Elder, Healer, or Knowledge Keeper in accordance with the protocols of the nation to which they belong. As such, I have not included teachings shared with me that might be considered sacred. The knowledge found within this book should be considered only within the context in which it is provided: in a relational dialogue between one teacher and one learner. Much care has gone into ensuring the teachings shared here are delivered with respect and as they were intended to be heard from the teacher who shared them with me.

A danger in integration work like this is that Western psychology can be assimilating; it can and has been used to replace or exploit Indigenous wellness frameworks for a long time. There is always also a risk of appropriation and misuse of Indigenous knowledges in a way that does not benefit or even harms Indigenous Peoples. To perpetuate colonization in this way would be gravely counterproductive. It is my hope instead to draw upon the strengths of both of these worlds to enhance our helping work, not replace it.

This book is not a manual, and it's not a curriculum. It's a gathering of memories, relationships, and practices, a way of holding what I've been given in gratitude, in hopes that it might be shared to help others as it has helped me. The teachings come from my own experience and from visits with family and Knowledge Keepers who have been generous enough to share what they felt I was ready to hear. These conversations happened at kitchen tables, on the road, in Ceremony, on the phone, at gatherings, and on the land. I've done my best to write them as I remember and understand them, always with respect for the context in which they were shared. Each of the Elders provided consent, reviewed, and approved of what is shared on these pages. That said, I do not claim to speak for anyone but myself. The teachings are shared with you in a spirit of humility, rather than as expertise or a fixed or universal truth. I've endeavoured to convey what I've learned in a way that also reflects my own story, my work as a helper, and the love and responsibility I feel towards those who have trusted me with their words. While I have taken great care to ensure their voices are represented with integrity, any mistakes are mine alone.

But why a book? Couldn't I just leave well enough alone, do therapy with Indigenous folks and keep things simple? Absolutely. That was the plan until I met an Elder named Ananias Spence. A few years back, I was presenting some of these ideas at an Indigenous education conference in Thunder Bay, Ontario. Ananias, an Anishinaabe Grandfather and highly respected Elder, had offered the opening prayer to start the day and then was seated in the row directly in front of me. Throughout my talk, I became very aware of Ananias's attention. His gaze was fixed on me, and he seemed to be listening to each word intently. This made me all sorts of nervous, but I trudged forward, having abandoned my electrolyte, pretzels, and compression sock routine several years prior.

After the talk finished, while I was packing up my things, Ananias's daughter approached me and said, "Hi there, my dad is wondering if he can have a copy of your book." I told her I didn't have a book, but that there were some great books that had inspired me that I would be happy to ship to her father. She smiled, thanked me, and then walked away. About ten minutes later, while I was about to leave, Ananias approached me himself. English was not his first language, and Ojibwe is not mine, but we managed. He was again asking for a copy of *my book*. I was super confused now but did my best to again explain that I didn't have a book, I had never written one, but that I would send him one he might like. He didn't appear interested in that and repeated, "*Your* book," now pointing his finger at me. I wasn't sure how to respond, so I politely thanked him and said, "I suppose I should set to work on writing something, eh?" He smiled and walked back to his seat, and I left the conference replaying that moment over and over again in my head. The day I got home from the conference, I sat down to write the first page of this book. And so here we are. Ananias began his journey to the spirit world in October of 2024. I wish I could have thanked him in person and told him how much this simple interaction changed my life. But until I make my own journey, I will have to send my thanks to him along with my prayers.

My guess is that if you've picked up this book, there's a good chance you're wrestling with something heavy. Maybe you're feeling disconnected from your family, community, or culture. Or you feel like you're caught between two worlds and don't quite fit in either one of them. Or maybe you're holding a deep sadness that keeps pulling you under, and the thought that the world might be better without you has started to whisper its way into the pit of your stomach. Maybe like me, the spirit of anxiety has wrapped itself tight across your chest, making it hard to catch your breath. It could be that the things you are using to get some relief or to numb the pain of trauma, loneliness, family conflict, and loss are starting to become their own problems. You might be deep in the grips of addiction or just starting to consider that substances may be damaging your relationships and your health. Maybe you're just trying to make sense of this strange, beautiful, and sometimes broken world and searching for where you might fit in it. Whatever brought you here, know that you're not alone. We're all out here trying to figure this thing out, and mostly scrambling along. To be clear, this book isn't going to give you all the answers—I sure as hell don't have them. But what I can offer is a part of me, the good, bad, and ugly, that you might find useful in marking your path. My hope in writing this book is that it will be of use to all those who are reaching for something. This includes you, your family, and your community.

For Indigenous readers, these teachings and stories may feel like coming home, a reconnection with the kind of healing wisdom that has carried our people for millennia. But why include the science of psychological flexibility at all? Why muddy the waters with a Western approach to wellness? On my own healing journey and while walking with others on theirs, I've found that this particular approach has a remarkable synergy with Indigenous perspectives of wellness. Those who have found healing in traditional teachings will likely find it interesting to see that in some ways, Western psychological science is finally catching up to what your grandmother was saying all along. And those who have found healing in Western psychological methods may find that these approaches are improved and enriched by the cultural context provided here and by the stories and practices of your unique culture.

While it is true that I have written this book primarily with my First Nations relatives in mind, I hold the teaching that all of us humans are relatives, and I believe that our helping wisdom can be of great benefit to people from every race and walk of life. After all, kahkithaw niwāhkōmākanitik, *all my relations*, doesn't mean "all my relations who look and speak like me." It means "*all my relations.*" So whoever you are, this book is also for you. I only ask that you treat the teachings you find here with the same respect and consideration that you would the precious stories of your own grandparents and great-grandparents.

Writing this book wasn't easy. If you've spent any time with a gifted Elder or Knowledge Keeper, you've likely learned to listen with patience and to let go of the urge to control the content, structure, and pace of learning. Quite a few times early in my learning and healing journey, I had a list of questions that I wanted to ask an Elder. I had a preconceived notion of what the answers might be, and I expected them to confirm that I was correct or to tell me how and why I was incorrect. I wanted to learn something new, but I wanted it to be delivered in a way that was most convenient and familiar for me. I wanted it to fit into the little learning checklist in my head, and I wanted it to be quick. This is a product of the colonized consciousness Leroy Little Bear spoke of and a system that tells us that the best way to learn is to sit at attention in a little desk for forty hours a week, to read and regurgitate words out of large textbooks, and to stand at the front of a class and repeat what we have read to our fellow zombies. This really is not natural. We were never meant to live or learn this way.

For thousands and thousands of years, we learned by throwing big rocks into a frozen river, by wrestling each other in the dirt, by watching animals scurry up trees and clouds shape-shift across the sky. We learned from our dreams and visions. We watched our siblings, cousins, uncles, aunties, grandparents, and great-grandparents build fires, cook, solve problems, manage conflicts, and share their memories with great peals of laughter. We learned by teaching and helping one another. Whether or not it fits in the most popular pedagogical model of the moment, we really learn within complex ecological systems, not in neat sequential modules.

The gifted Knowledge Keepers know this, and they are keen not to simply give you something to regurgitate. This is why you often don't get the answer you're hoping for when speaking to an Elder. Instead, you get the answer that you need to hear at that time and place. Sometimes this means being told the same story or concept over and over again. I used to think that some of the Elders I spoke with simply forgot that they had told me the story before, until one of them quipped, "I think this is maybe the twelfth time I've told you that one. Maybe this time you'll hear it." It turned out I was being the redundant one in my failure to identify the relationships they were quite clearly pointing out for me. Indigenous pedagogy is a bit like a spiral, where you pass over teachings again and again in your journey towards understanding at changing levels of context. So if something seems like it is being repeated over and over, it's most likely for a reason; either you need to hear it again to understand it for the first time, or you need to hear it again to apply it in the new context you find yourself in.

I've also come to understand that many Knowledge Keepers share with you only what they think you are ready for and what will be most helpful for you at that particular time in your life. This can be frustrating for those who have spent a lifetime being spoon-fed information and praised for simply remembering it out loud. It may also mean that you are unlikely to be given some direct solution to your problem. You putting things together yourself for your unique context is more valuable than simply knowing it and trying to replicate a series of steps exactly how someone else did. Great therapists take a similar approach; they rarely tell you what they think something means or what you should do about it. I know I've wanted to shake my therapist a few times and scream, "Just tell me what to do already!" I'm sure the people I work with have wanted to shake me for this reason too; I don't blame them. Good helpers know that they don't have the answers, but they're willing to walk with you and not look away while you find your own.

Another challenge comes from the tendency of many Elders to "think in Indian" (to borrow the words of Haudenosaunee philosopher and activist John Mohawk). What I mean by this is that there is often more focus on the relationship between concepts than on causal factors (why they happened), their sequences (what order they happened in), or the outcomes (what results or changes were generated from them). This relational understanding emphasizes the interconnectedness of things, the broader implications of actions and events, and the relevance of space and place, rather than simply analyzing individual elements in isolation or neat linear progressions. This can be disorienting for those who are accustomed to more systematic and predictable methods of problem-solving and reasoning.

A simple question might result in a very broad (and sometimes long) discussion of many related concepts. Some Elders and Knowledge Keepers will branch out in many directions before returning to the topic, some might not return to the initial topic at all. By focusing on the many relationships between concepts rather than their structure or sequences, the teachings encourage a more expansive reflection and integration of knowledge, urging us to see beyond the surface and appreciate the complexity and its relevance in the context of our own lives. I didn't realize it at first, but this is an incredible way to promote psychological flexibility while combating the rigidity that our modernized minds crave and that tends to get us stuck in problematic patterns.

While writing this book, I did my best to resist the urge to fit the teachings into neat little boxes or lists, or to spoon-feed them to you in an overly digestible manner. Instead, I present the teachings as they were given to me, with the relationship prioritized over the structure or sequence. At the same time, I did want the book to be of practical use in your helping and healing journey, so I have provided my own reflections as an opportunity for you to explore these concepts for yourself in real time. The result is a journey where at times you walk with the Knowledge Keepers and sometimes with me, and other times you walk with your own spirit and with your spirit helpers. You never walk alone. As you explore this book, I encourage you to approach the readings with willingness and curiosity, using your own experiences to determine what resonates with you, what holds meaning, and how it aligns (or doesn't align) with your own worldview and what you want your life to be about. As I often hear the old ones say, "Take what you need and leave the rest behind."

* * *

Let's get going.

OTŌTĪMOWIN

The tree stands in all sorts of weather and never complains; if you're not bending like that, you're going to break.

Grandmother Renée Thomas-Hill

1.

OTŌTĪMOWIN

Otōtīmowin is a word in nēhiyawīwin (the Plains Cree dialect) that speaks to a way of being that is open-hearted, relational, and available to others. Simon Bird, a gifted language teacher from Southend Reindeer Lake, Saskatchewan, told me that while the meaning is highly dependent on context, *otōtīmowin* can be understood as a way of being approachable, willing to connect, and ready to be in relationship. It may be used to describe people who are warm and attentive, someone who greets others with genuine interest, who makes space for conversation, who is not guarded or withdrawn. To be described with the term *otōtīmowin* is a sign of someone who interacts in a good way with others.

When you examine the word more closely, you find that it refers to the quality or condition of belonging through kinship. Its root, *otōtēma*, speaks to one's clan or family lineage. The suffix *-win* gives it shape as a state of being. Together, they form a word that speaks to relational identity, an understanding of the self through community, land, and ancestry.

The word also carries a deeper teaching. It can serve as a guide for how we relate not only to other people, but also to the full range of experiences that live around us and within us. This way of being is one that makes room for all our experiences in their natural form.

This includes our thoughts, feelings, physical sensations, and memories. Some are light, pleasant, and easy to carry. Others feel heavy, sharp, or tangled. Applied in the context of being a good relative to our own experiences, the teaching invites us to welcome them all in with compassion and curiosity, rather than our usual approach of shoving them away or doing our best to keep them hidden.

There are many ways we learn to step away from what hurts. We keep ourselves busy. We reach for substances to soften the painful edges. We scroll our phones until the world fades away, or repeat positive affirmations to silence the critical voices rising inside. Sometimes we seek comfort through control, reassurance, food, or meticulous planning. These responses often come from a place of care. They arise from patterns built to protect us. At the same time, they can pull us away from the teachings our discomfort is offering. When we take a stance of willingness rather than defence, we are invited into a different kind of relationship with those experiences. We meet what comes with a soft front. We let it sit down. We put some tea on. We listen.

This way of being does not arrive all at once. It is something we grow into. It is a skill like practising the guitar or learning to drive. Mastery comes through repeated, undefended contact with our inner and outer worlds. In the pages that follow, I will introduce you to some Knowledge Keepers who have shared teachings that I think embody this way of being. But first, some time travel and a question most of us have asked at our most difficult moments.

TRAPLINES AND TIME TRAVEL

"Mósom, why do we suffer?" The lake is glass-still and paints a second sky upside down in the water.

"Well, what comes to mind when you hear the word *pain*?" I

hear my grandfather say from beside the fire where he is cleaning a long, skinny jackfish, parsing out the troublesome Y-bones with ease. We share the same name, but I sadly did not inherit his fish-cleaning skills. He is speaking Old Cree, but in the dream, I am able to understand everything he says completely.

"Pain?" I parrot, letting the word settle in as he slides the round knife over the tough, slimy skin, separating a perfect fillet that wastes nothing. I set down the branches and the brush I had been collecting and put my hands on my hips. "Uh, hurt?" I stammer. Now he is flipping the fish over and cutting under the gills and around the pectoral fin. "Cut?" I try. Still nothing. "Bad, trauma, injury, suffering, wound?"

He looks up only briefly and points his lips at the bucket beside me. I hand it over to him as he tosses in the fillet, splashing my leg with the fishy water. This makes him smile.

"And what else?" He pulls the next fish out from the black tub beside him and starts the process all over.

"Sickness? Fear? Burn?" As the words come out, I feel a sinking in my stomach and a flood of memory that makes me recoil inward. "Death?" I say. I can feel a lump forming in my throat, and I suddenly don't want to play this game anymore.

"Mmm-hmm," he says, neither agreeing nor disagreeing, just acknowledging that he has heard me. He's on his third fish now, and I know that he has already given me his answer, but I don't yet understand.

As I wake up, I can still smell the fire burning.

THE GREAT EQUALIZER

Across a lifetime, every person will encounter moments of injury, illness, loss, frustration, failure, and heartbreak. With time, we also come to face the realities of aging bodies, changing capacities, the deaths of people we love, and, eventually, our own mortality. In this sense, pain may be one of the few experiences that genuinely connects us, a shared thread that runs beneath differences of culture, belief, and circumstance.

Pain does not come only from what happens around us. The world inside of us can also be a wellspring for much pain. Fear, grief, shame, anger, worry, and loneliness show up regularly in ordinary life. Our minds are capable of producing thoughts that feel harsh, critical, or overwhelming. While these experiences are often uncomfortable, they are not signs that something has gone wrong. Throughout human history, pain arising both from our environment and from within ourselves has shaped how people learn, adapt, and survive.

These experiences have always required response and ingenuity. Pain has demanded attention, learning, and change. In this way, it has played a role in the development of ways of living that support endurance and care, both individually and collectively.

Long before the arrival of Europeans and the violence that followed, Indigenous Peoples on Turtle Island lived with the realities of war, injury, disease, loss, and the challenges of harsh environments. These experiences were never sought out, but they required adaptation, learning, and ingenuity in the face of uncertainty. Across countless generations, our ancestors did more than persist. They developed complex systems of governance, language, education, art, spirituality, and medicine that supported life, health, and meaning over long periods of time, even amid sustained attempts to erase them.

Because of this long relationship with hardship, many Indigenous teachings speak about pain differently than dominant cultural narratives often do. Pain is understood as part of being alive, not as a personal failure or something that automatically signals something has gone wrong. In this respect, the science of psychological flexibility aligns closely with the teachings shared by many Indigenous helpers and Knowledge Keepers I have had the privilege to learn from. Both recognize that while pain is unavoidable, how we relate to it can shape how we live.

GRANDMOTHER RENÉE THOMAS-HILL

The first stop on our journey brings us to the lands of the great Haudenosaunee Confederacy along the mighty Grand River and to the kitchen table of Grandmother Renée Thomas-Hill. Grandmother Renée is a Cayuga Bear and Turtle Clan Elder of the Mohawk Nation. She is a gifted healer, counsellor, storyteller, educator, historian, lecturer, agriculturalist, and artisan doll maker. She has had a remarkable career spanning many decades and cares deeply for her people. Grandmother Renée peers out at you from behind her glasses with kind eyes and a soft, welcoming smile, but don't let that fool you! She's a no-nonsense kōhkom who doesn't mince her words and always gives it to you straight. I really enjoyed getting to know Grandmother Renée and felt an immediate comfort and security in her presence.

In our first visit together, Grandmother Renée described pain as a message from spirit, a wake-up call with the capacity to remind us that we are sacred and to reorient us towards needs we may be neglecting. From her perspective, physical and emotional pain are valuable teachers that help the different parts of ourselves communicate more effectively. I remember her sharing a teaching that has stayed with me. She described the heart, the body, the mind, and the spirit as members of a family, each with its own voice and wisdom.

Our heart, the place where we feel the full spectrum of our emotions, is the Grandmother of this family. The Grandmother is wise and is often the first to know that something is wrong. The Grandmother is also the source of self-compassion, the one who reminds us that we are worthy of love and safety by birthright.

The body is the Mother. Like the Grandmother, the body is concerned with our well-being and sends reminders and makes us aware of what we need to be well.

Our spirit is our Great-Grandmother. While science and psychology have become better at seeing the interconnection of mind, body, and emotion, spirit is still dismissed as belonging to some category outside of health care; this is a mistake. Grandmother Renée insists that our spirit is always speaking to us. We may call it intuition, a gut feeling, or our conscience, but spirit is that part of us that is intimately connected to every other aspect of reality. Grandmother Renée's own grandmother used to refer to spirit as our "crap detector," that part of us that intuitively knows the difference between right and wrong, knows when something is "off," and lets us know when we are bumping up against our values or the natural laws.

Our mind is the Child of our family. The mind is curious and energetic, but impulsive and often too busy thinking of its own needs to listen to what Mother, Grandmother, or Great-Grandmother has to say. Grandmother Renée warns that when we give our mind all the power in the absence of any sort of structure or discipline, we soon run into problems. When our childlike mind strays too far from those other parts of us, it can become destructive and inadvertently cause itself and the others harm. Then, when it inevitably runs into trouble, the mind frantically searches for ways to make things better, but its foresight is limited, so often it seeks out the most immediate sources of relief while ignoring the advice of Mother/body and Grandmother/heart, who plead for a slower, more measured approach to healing. By pausing and paying attention to what our heart and body are saying, our mind is given an opportunity to make an informed decision, and to ask questions about what matters most. Like sitting and working something out with a loving grandparent who has been where we are before.

Stop for a moment and see if you can hear what each member of your family is saying right now. I know how easy it would be to skip ahead when you read the words *stop for a moment and* . . . in a book like this. It may feel weird or hokey; I get that. If you do skip ahead, know that it's okay, maybe you will come back around to it, but know that you might be leaving something valuable behind, and that's also okay if you're okay with it. If, however, you are willing to sit in a little weirdness for a moment, go ahead and notice what each member of your inner family is saying right now—even if it's just their reaction to the invitation to this exercise.

If you pause and listen, you will likely hear the Child mind speak up first, impulsive and impatient, and a series of thoughts will eventually spring into your head about what you are going to have for dinner or about a bill that you haven't paid yet. Maybe your mind will toss a memory your way, or pass some judgment on what you have read thus far. It will most certainly have something to say about this strange sitting-and-listening activity I am proposing. In fact, it's likely that as you've been reading these words, your mind has already piped in with distractions or criticisms at least a few times. Mine certainly has while writing them. Just take a moment to be curious and observe whatever your mind does.

Now what about the Mother? For a moment, see if you can really listen to your body, start at the top of your head and slowly work your way down, noting any sensation that is there: an itch, tension, soreness, whatever. Notice temperature, pressure, movement, or stillness.

Finally, listen to Grandmother. What feelings are present? What does your heart say? This one is the most difficult, as Grandmothers tend to speak very softly. I often hear from my emotions first in my chest and throat, but the experience of emotion is complex and very subjective. Emotion involves a wide range of physiological and psychological experiences, and the exact way you experience what your mind has labelled sadness or worry is likely different from mine. In fact, for all its incredible feats, modern science has yet to come to a consensus of what emotions actually are. But each of us intimately knows the weight of heartache after a loss, the sharp sting of anger after having been betrayed, or the radiating warmth at reuniting with a loved one after a long absence. Just because we feel doesn't mean that we are able to recognize, describe, or communicate our emotions effectively; many of us really struggle to do this. To complicate matters, we are frequently so distracted by our mind running wild that we fail to pay any attention to our hearts. Sometimes everyone else in the room is aware of our emotional state before we are.

As you sit here now, what do you feel in your heart? Perhaps there is a dull sadness or some latent fear, a mild irritability, impatience, or restlessness; maybe there is a numbness or a warm contentment or a deep feeling of peace. No need to judge or try to change what you feel; just notice anything that comes up. Spirit, the Great-Grandmother of our system, speaks to each of us in different ways. I recall my cousin Terrance saying that it is up to each of us to determine how our spirit speaks to us, depending on the unique gifts we have been given. Whether it be through dream or vision, through signs in nature, in Ceremony, a voice in stillness, or some other medium, the spirit's journey is a personal one that takes a lifetime of listening and nurturing.

Listening to our heart, body, and spirit can be difficult when our mind is commanding the spotlight all the time. It's like trying to have a quiet conversation with your cousin on the bus while the person beside you is yelling at the top of their lungs into their phone. Grandmother Renée once compared the mind to a runaway horse. I remember her telling me how hard it can be to grab the reins when the mind starts its bucking and galloping. "You have to pull back, slow the horse down, and get it started back in the direction of your destination, which can be tough with a horse that has yet to receive any training," she says.

Grandmother Renée often emphasizes the role of language in our pursuit of the good life, that words both spoken and thought have the capacity to cause significant suffering. Certain words and phrases in particular bother Grandmother Renée, including the use of profanity, words that communicate indifference ("I don't care"), conceit ("Mine, mine, mine!"), or stubbornness ("I will only do it my way"). She says that the language of hatred and anger shows us that someone is hanging on tightly to their grief, so much so that it comes pouring out of them. She insists that using these words is like putting our own hand in a fire to hurt someone else.

I laughed when Grandmother Renée shared the teaching of the squirrel who tells on you when you use your words inappropriately. The squirrel sits up high in the tree and listens, and when it hears those hurtful words, it rings out with its loud chirping, almost making a "Tsk, tsk, tsk!" sound that a Grandmother might make when she sees you doing something you shouldn't be doing. I chuckled when I heard this because it is something that both my mom and nōhkom used to say when I was a kid. I'd be climbing a tree or swinging a stick around and suddenly get blasted by an angry squirrel, which would scare the heck out of me, and inevitably my mom, auntie, or nōhkom would say, "Oh! What have you been up to? Were you swearing? The squirrels are telling on you!" I always thought they were just being a bit nuts (pun intended), but it turns out, just like my Cree granny from South Indian Lake, Mohawk grannies three thousand kilometres southeast were also warning their grandchildren about snitching squirrels.

Grandmother Renée is pointing towards something essential here. How we live with pain and suffering is shaped not only by what happens to us, but by how we make sense of those experiences. Language plays a central role in that process. The ways we describe, label, and organize what we go through influences how pain manifests in our bodies and lives.

Human minds are built for relationship. We notice patterns, draw links, and hold things together across time. Our capacity for language allows us to connect what we see, hear, and feel with memories, expectations, and meanings that exist beyond the present moment. Much of this happens automatically, without deliberate effort or awareness.

This ability has been vital for creativity, problem-solving, and survival. At the same time, it brings a particular vulnerability. Because we can form rich connections between experiences, we can be affected by things that are not actually happening right now. A remembered image, a familiar phrase, or a brief thought can carry the weight of a lived event. A pleasant memory with someone who has died can arrive with such force that grief floods the body, as if we were standing at their funeral again.

If our capacity for language can draw us into these painful

moments, it may also offer a way forward. The same processes that bind us to suffering can be worked with differently, opening space for new ways of relating to pain rather than being overtaken by it.

A fundamental teaching for the Mohawk people is that of the Good Mind. Grandmother Renée spoke of this often during our visits. The Good Mind is a philosophy that promotes an awareness of our thoughts and the intentions behind them. When we view our thoughts with patience and carefully examine the words and explore their possible source and impact on others, we can respond with love and kindness. This promotes peace, a particularly important value in the Mohawk worldview. Practising the way of the Good Mind is also about finding balance in body, mind, heart, and spirit. It is about being in harmony with all things in Creation.

Unlike many of the contemplative practices found in contemporary mindfulness psychologies, however, the Good Mind is not viewed as an individualistic or exclusively introspective activity, but a practice that binds people together in a spirit of peace and collaboration. During the Thanksgiving Address that opens many Haudenosaunee events and ceremonies, the words *our minds are one* are repeated while giving thanks to all aspects of Creation. The philosophy of the Good Mind is complex and based on many teachings and stories that are best sought out in relationship with an Elder or Knowledge Keeper rather than read here in a book. So if this is of interest to you, consider offering a gift to a Knowledge Holder from one of the great Haudenosaunee nations.

Grandmother Renée believes that our mind tests us at every moment. It loves categories and dualities, and wants to label things as this or that, good or bad. She shares a teaching of the twins in all of us, a voice that encourages us and another that seems to want to bring us down. One voice will say, "Woah, we're nervous! This is a big deal! This is not good! We are going to fail!" and the other will say, "Calm down. Everything is fine. Everything will be okay. We've been preparing for this!" And we go back and forth like this, trying to find some consensus between the two, which can be chaotic and exhausting.

Grandmother Renée doesn't see the twins as good and evil, however, but describes them both as guards and helpers. The goal isn't to get rid of one or the other or for one or the other to win, she says. That's impossible and not actually in our best interest. When the twins come together, they can create something beautiful. But first we need to calm the noise we are bringing in response and find enough peace in the moment to actually hear what they are saying and why.

These teachings share some things in common with the psychological flexibility approach. Viewing our thoughts with patience and curiosity can create some distance from them, allowing us to "de-fuse" from them. When we get stuck to our thoughts, we allow them to direct our behaviour, we take them at face value as absolute truth, and they tend to monopolize our attention, causing us to miss out on all the beauty that Creation has to offer.

"So what can we do?" I ask. I'd love Grandmother Renée to give me the secret to a silent mind, but I'd settle for a way to shut my meaner twin up once in a while.

"Do?" she says, looking at me like I've got two heads now. "Maybe it's all the doing that's your problem." Now she is studying the confused look on my face. "When you notice those inner energies engaged in their tug-of-war, you might try a different approach than proving one right or wrong, or seeking that escape and immediate comfort." Grandmother Renée says, "What if, just for a moment, you could see these thoughts with the curiosity of a young child looking up and seeing a rainbow or fireworks for the first time? Simply acknowledging, 'Oh, that's an interesting thought!' without needing to agree, disagree, or judge it in any way?"

I find it hard to imagine myself looking at some of my more difficult and self-critical thoughts this way, but as usual, Grandmother Renée has a story that burns the teaching into my brain.

"Yesterday, this thought flew onto my windowsill as I was lying down for a nap," she says, wiggling her shoulders to demonstrate the arrogant way the bird strutted into her bedroom. "It had the most interesting colours, and it was very noisy, which made it hard for me to sleep. And to make things worse, it kept saying these terrible things were going to happen. I tried to shoo it away, but it just got louder and louder and meaner and scarier in the things it was saying," she says, her expression demonstrating how annoyed she was at this. "I tried to ignore it, but then a second thought flew in and landed right beside the first one. This one was so unique looking, with bright tail feathers and a little fuzzy ball on its head. It was squawking at the other thought about how everything was going to be okay and telling me that I shouldn't worry.

"As I watched and listened to this loud discussion they were having, I noticed they were almost dancing with each other, wings and tail feathers going up and down and side to side like this"—another demonstration with her shoulders. "Finally I sat back and just watched the show they were putting on for me. How lucky I was to have such colourful visitors. And then I noticed that when I stopped trying to shoo them away, they quieted a bit, they were still there arguing back and forth, but before too long I was drifting off to sleep anyway."

I think I know what she's getting at, but still the question bounces around in my head: And then what? Grandmother Renée sees me floundering.

"Let me tell it another way," she says with a patient smile.

"Growing up along the river, you learn everything about the water when you're very little," she says. "You form an intimate connection with the river." She pulls gently at the colourful kōhkom shawl draped over her shoulders, seeing something else entirely in her memory:

> My grandmother used to say, "You see those green grasses in the water? Those lake grasses are like hands; sometimes they are waving at you, but you must be careful." When you are out swimming, those grasses might touch your legs and frighten you. Maybe you had a cramp and slowed for a moment to rest and then experienced a jolt of terror at the long, slimy hands touching you. Sometimes those hands can wrap around you, keep you stuck. And of course, you panic and struggle, kick your legs and flap your arms in a wild effort to escape, but all this does is get you even more tangled in even more of the long, grassy fingers. Now it feels like they are pulling you down, down, down. It's like this with anxiety, isn't it? When a thought comes, it might frighten you and stop you right in your tracks. And your first urge will be to kick and scream and fight to get away, but this just gets us more of the same. You have to learn to float instead.

As with the watchful squirrels of my youth, Grandmother Renée seems to have tapped into some long-buried memory database on this one.

It's summer, and I'm maybe ten years old, probably rocking purple jogging pants with neon lightning bolts on them and a pretty deadly rattail to go with them. We had made the fifteen-hour drive up to Lynn Lake from Winnipeg a few weeks earlier. I often wonder how my parents managed not to kill any of us during those long, dusty trips up Highway 391. We were visiting in South Indian Lake, and my cousin Donnie (also called Junior back then) and I had found two large Styrofoam tubs at the fish plant and taken them out by the cliffs to use as makeshift rowboats. The tubs were in pretty rough shape, so it wasn't quite as elegant as you might imagine. It was more like straddling a half-floating piece of fish-smelling refuse while trying to propel ourselves with broken oars and pieces of wood we had found on the way down the bank. Aesthetics aside, we were doing pretty well and had made it around the point when we passed over a jungle of dark-green seaweed.

The water in South Indian Lake is a sort of pastel blue and difficult to see very far into, as flooding caused by hydroelectric damming has resulted in severe erosion and chemical imbalances, including the synthesis of the neurotoxin methylmercury. For ten-year-old me, the combination of the deep, opaque, oddly coloured water and the long green salad fingers reaching out to tickle my feet made for a truly horrifying experience.

I immediately started kicking and paddling frantically in an attempt to escape. In what I can only imagine was some divine punishment for swearing at squirrels, my Styrofoam raft cracked in half, plunging me into the depths of the killer kelp. My pasty city-boy arms and legs flailed wildly, and I half screamed, half gurgled for help as my life flashed before my eyes. The long strands did indeed appear to be wrapping around me and pulling me down towards whatever sea creatures lurk below. I was a very good swimmer—we swam for five or six hours a day until we were pruney beyond recognition—but at this moment I felt as if it were the first time I had ever touched water.

Just as I resigned myself to a dark fate in the depths off the point, I felt an old boat rope touch my hand and pulled myself up. My cousin Donnie, who at first looked astonished by the scene I was making, proceeded to break out in loud, cackling laughter as he towed me towards the shore. Donnie was two years younger than me but had grown up in the bush and seemed like he was never afraid. To him, the seaweed was just another beautiful part of the adventure. I didn't know it then, and if I did, I'm sure I did my best not to show it, but I learned a lot from my cousins when we visited the North.

I thank Grandmother Renée and leave her with broadcloth and tobacco in a large, brightly coloured sewing chest in gratitude for the teachings she has shared so openly. Driving home alongside the vibrant beauty of the Grand River in the cold lull of autumn, I find myself reflecting on the many species of seaweed I have struggled against in my life. An old one that still likes to wrap its long green arms around me every now and then is the thought and feeling that I have done something wrong and that someone is angry at me as a result. For many years I have kicked my legs and thrashed my arms violently to prove these intrusive and unwanted thoughts wrong, to distract myself from them, to attack their source, to escape them in any way I can. This has involved replaying positive narratives over and over in my mind in the hopes of convincing my thoughts they are wrong, seeking reassurance and approval from others, and trying to do a whole bunch of "right" things to bury the perceived wrongs.

It has taken me much too long to realize that not only have these strategies been ineffective, they have only served to pull me further down into the grasp of those long green strands of self-deprecation. The more I attempted to fight the unwanted thoughts, the more I thought about them, and the more of my time and attention they commanded. Even when I was thinking "positive thoughts," the critical ones were lurking just behind them. Whenever I tried to prove myself as "good," the thoughts were waiting close by to whisper, "But not enough." Whenever I attacked them head-on, they hit back much harder. And even when I was able to numb or distract myself with substances or heavy metal or work, it was typically a very short-lived solution.

While I will admit I still feel the sting of fear when passing over the seaweed in my life, and even get caught up kicking at them from time to time, more and more I'm learning to float, and to see them for what they are: another interesting, even beautiful part of this human journey we're on.

In the very short time spent with Grandmother Renée, I have learned so much, but have also become painfully aware of all that I do not know. The journey has just begun.

2.

LEN PIERRE

Now we head west, over our great stone Grandfathers, through giant redwood forests, to the oceanside territory of the Coast Salish Peoples and to the cozy living room of Len Pierre. Len is a Coast Salish consultant from Katzie First Nation. His work includes public speaking, education, cultural practice, and what he describes as being a spiritual gangster. Len is one of those charismatic spirits who carries an energy so bright, you'll want to listen to him speak for hours without blinking. And Len is a busy fella. If he isn't doing a TED Talk or giving a motivational speech to a group of youths, he's doing yoga or training organizations on Indigenous harm reduction, leadership, cultural awareness, or lateral violence prevention. I was thrilled when Len agreed to visit with me and was eager to absorb whatever knowledge he was willing to share.

I tell Len about my chat with Grandmother Renée and about the parallels I have been seeing in traditional teachings on the good life and the psychological flexibility approach to wellness. I ask Len what he thinks about pain, a bit of a weird question to kick a visit off, sure. He laughs and then settles into teacher mode.

Len shares that from a traditional perspective, pain has always been conceptualized as a very natural human experience, similar to birth and death. Something not to be avoided, but to be expected. He describes the experience of pain as "intimate, natural, and fluid." These are not words that I had previously associated with the word *pain*. Len points to our tendency to ascribe arbitrary labels to our experiences, especially binaries like "good and bad" and "right and wrong." And of course, we then try our best to resist and control those things we've labelled bad or wrong. Len's opinion is that this dualistic way of thinking and labelling things as "either or" represents a colonial mindset. To Len, the idea that we can have bad, wrong, irrational, or incorrect emotions or thoughts is reductionistic and not in line with the wholistic and integrative worldview of the Coast Salish Peoples. He argues that emotions do not and cannot exist on a linear continuum with joy on one side and sorrow on the other, but instead move fluidly within a complex network that shoots around and across a never-ending circle.

Len points to the danger of resisting our difficult experiences and compares the processing of physical, emotional, mental, and spiritual pain to a natural function like digestion. To Len, these difficult experiences have important nutrients that we need to take from them to help us grow. But we also need to allow them to pass through our bodies to make way for new experiences. When we attempt to control those experiences, they stay with us and make us sick.

This may seem counterintuitive. How could the crushing sadness I feel after losing a loved one possibly be nourishing? What teachings could this unbearable grief possibly provide me with? But even these difficult experiences are important. Our experience of sadness tells us to slow down, rest, and recuperate. Our grief orients us towards what is most important in our lives and reminds us how much we loved someone. Our anger asserts our needs, sets boundaries, and protects our relationships. And most often, these difficult experiences alert us to something that needs to change in our lives.

"Our emotions are a signal," says Len. "Fear, anxiety, sadness, or disgust; they are a flashing temperature gauge, a sign it's time to take a look under the hood." Len is right. Emotions can have the powerful effect of mobilizing us for action. While in the moment, emotions like sadness and its many cousins (loneliness, numbness, disappointment, heartbreak, exhaustion, and grief) may feel like an incredible weight on your shoulders, they too can be a motivating force to seek help and to do things differently.

Len's teaching invites us to sit with these inner signals in a new way. "What vital messages might anger be trying to deliver in our lives?" he asks. "How has sadness, in its quiet way, perhaps pointed us towards what truly needs our care and attention?"

I think about the difficult emotions I have wrestled with over the last few years, the anger, fear, and sadness, and I try to think on what purpose each one has attempted to serve in my life. Len says they're attempting to deliver a message, but we keep dodging their phone calls. And yes, these messengers can make a big mess of things. It's like they're trying to deliver a pamphlet about lawn-care but end up trampling all your flowers and knocking over a garbage can on the way to your mailbox.

Anger arrived for me when I needed to set a clear boundary in my relationships. Grief visited to say it was okay to pause as I transitioned into a new part of my life.

"Maybe these aren't problems to be solved; they are parts of your story just waiting to be acknowledged," Len says. Damn, he's wise. I sometimes think an old man got himself trapped in Len's young-man body somehow.

As we continue to chat, I notice that rather than saying things like "depressed people" or "when I am anxious" or "mentally ill," Len describes these experiences as "being in relationship with anxiety" or "finding ourselves in a relationship with depression." I find this really interesting and wonder if it may be a function of the polysynthetic nature of many Indigenous languages.

While English is largely noun-based, with relatively few morphemes, a lot of Indigenous languages in North America are highly verb-based, with many affixes that significantly modify tense, mood, and direction. This means that even simple words cannot be translated without being aware of the context, the relationship of the speaker to the listener, and their relationship to the subject matter. Even the mood and intention of the speaker matter when deciding how to say something.

Because of this, whenever I ask my mom for what I think will be a simple translation like how to say "a grumpy cat" in nīhithawīwin, she blitzes me with twenty questions: Whose cat is it? What is the cat doing? Who are you talking to? Why are you talking about a cat? Why is it grumpy? While it makes translation tricky, it allows for an incredible amount of meaning and a rich network of relationships and associations. For example, while there isn't really a word for "depression" as it is used as a noun in English, a comparable phrase in nīhithawīwin (the Woodland Cree dialect) might be ē-wanītēhīpathit, which would translate to a verb like "her heart has turned in the opposite direction." A dynamic interaction with the environment is built into the language itself, with each word containing a complex network of relationships and actions, which likely contributes to considerable flexibility for those who organize their thoughts in such ways.

By saying, "We have found ourselves in a relationship with depression," rather than "When we are depressed" or "When we have depression," whether he is aware of it or not, Len is leveraging the structure of Indigenous languages in the service of psychological flexibility. If I am in a relationship with a series of thoughts and emotions that are labelled by the Western pathology paradigm as depression, then *I am* not myself depressed, nor do *I have* depression in the sense that it is something foreign that has infected me like a virus. It is a visitor, and not necessarily one that we are trying to hurry out the door, but one that has come with an important message. Sometimes the most important messages we receive are incredibly painful.

I can't help but notice a dull ache in the pit of my stomach while writing this section. Perhaps regret for not learning more of my language from my fluent mother. I believe this to be one of the most damaging and enduring impacts of the genocide Indigenous Peoples have experienced in North America and around the world: the loss of language and the ability to think and speak in the language of relationship.

Len and I head out for a walk among the great Sitka spruce, red alder, and black cottonwood of Stanley Park, and I am transfixed by the beauty. The North is beautiful too, and I wouldn't trade it for any place in the world, but the territory of the Coast Salish Peoples is vibrant, diverse, and unmistakably alive. I have visited a handful of times over the years, but each time I come back, I find myself once again captured by the spectacle. Fall has not yet arrived here, and the breeze pulls the crisp scent of cedar and pine and a thick musk of moss into me. Suddenly I remember one of the questions I had intended to ask before getting distracted by Len's wisdom, which, like the summer breeze, seems to flow with such ease.

What does *wellness* mean? So often our focus is solely on pathology, it almost sounds like an absurd question to ask. As a society we have become experts in illness. The current edition of the *Diagnostic and Statistical Manual of Mental Disorders* (*DSM-5*) lists over 150 distinct diagnostic categories and nearly 300 specific disorders, and it is highly likely that the next edition will have many more. In today's system of social media diagnoses and fast-food-style psychiatric treatments, *wellness* simply means the absence of disease. But you can be disease-free and still not be well, can't you? And can't you be disordered and be well?

"Uy' sqwaluwun (ʔuy' sq̓ʷəluwun)," Len says. "A good heart and spirit, and a good flow in alignment." To be well means to be well aligned. There is a natural flow of wellness that comes to us from the land, from the water, from the animals and people; it is constantly bombarding us, but we can only accept that wellness *if* we are willing to feel fully and completely, he says. The work of wellness is in creating synergy and reconnection between our emotional, physical, mental, and spiritual selves. And that self is not restricted to our physical bodies, to a single person, or to human beings. The barrier between us and the universe is not as opaque as we think. We are permeable, but our big colonized brains make us forget it and convince us that we are an entity completely separate from nature. So in addition to creating it, the work of wellness is also about noticing the synergy and reconnection that already exists in the world around us. "Wellness comes easily if you let it," Len says. Goosebumps.

When speaking about how we can sit with difficult inner experiences such as intense anxiety or deep grief, Len talks about the importance of learning how to work with the mind. He often describes this as a form of training. In our cultures, he reminds me, we have always practised and prepared for what matters. We train for Ceremony, for survival, for leadership, and for responsibility. What seems to have faded, he suggests, is the idea that our thoughts and emotions can also be tended to and shaped with care. For generations, Ceremony created spaces where this kind of inner work could happen. Stillness, repetition, and ritual offered ways of bringing difficult experiences out of isolation and into relationship, where they could be understood differently.

Len shares that he sometimes works with heavy thoughts or feelings by writing them down and carrying them with him on the land. At times, he has placed stones marked with those experiences into a pack and walked with them into the mountains, releasing their weight into water when the moment feels right. At other times, he describes offering written thoughts or memories to the fire. As he once said, "Fire offers a pathway to acceptance." The intention is not to get rid of these experiences, but to honour them. Passing something through fire, Len explains, changes our relationship to it. It is given over, transformed, and no longer carried in the same way.

This teaching reminds me of how our relatives are understood to journey into the spirit world. They are not gone, but changed. In the same way, Len speaks about emotions, even the painful ones, as among the greatest gifts we are given. Our heart, he teaches, can guide us while we are alive, not so that we disappear from experience, but so that we learn how to be transformed by it.

"Our thoughts are not just thoughts," Len says. "We have spirits, powerful emotions, and incredible bodies that are all part of the same immutable whole." The idea that our thoughts are a distinct phenomenon all on their own only compartmentalizes the human experience, which is really not how things work. Len insists that we can't talk about our thoughts without talking about our bodies, our hearts, and our spirits. The separation is an illusion that gets us into all sorts of trouble.

The four quadrants are always in relationship and in flux with one another. To illustrate this, Len points to the many water teachings that the Coast Salish Peoples share. Many of these teachings provide important lessons on caring for our bodies, hearts, minds, and spirits. For example, Len shares that rather than being left or right, good or bad, right or wrong, our minds (along with our heart, body, and spirit) are more like a stream that flows through us. To think of the stream as separate from the plants it nourishes or the rocks that carry it isn't quite right. And to think of a single glass of that water as being a thing all on its own also isn't right. The stream is always in motion and always connecting things. I recall Grandmother Renée also making a connection between thought and water: "Our difficult experiences often represent a blockage. A big storm has come and gathered up all of the branches and logs in the river, and the passage for the water becomes more and more narrow, blocking the energy that is supposed to flow through our minds and bodies." I really love seeing the points of convergence in the teachings Len and Grandmother Renée shared. I feel like they would be good friends.

Looking at our thoughts as problematic can be overwhelming. All of us have hundreds if not thousands of challenging thoughts a day. Self-judgments, judgments of others, fears of the future, and bad memories are always just a thought away. By looking at this part of us as a problem, we create more and more barriers for ourselves. But we must remember that this is the same part of us that is creative, that plans, that communicates with others, that solves problems, that remembers beautiful moments, and that loves. We can't throw out those difficult experiences without throwing out all the good stuff with it; they are the same.

This isn't to say that we should just ignore our thoughts as unimportant. Len insists that thoughts carry a spiritual charge. Just as our words can wound or heal someone else, our thoughts can wound or heal us. "Thoughts carry a vibration, they carry power," Len says. "They are a gift." Len says that our thoughts are like dark clouds: "We know that they bring the rain that fills our rivers and spreads life throughout our worlds, but obviously we don't want it to always be cloudy; life also needs the sun. So when the rain and clouds are here, we don't shoo them away; we appreciate that they have a purpose, thank them, and remember that they will move on and the sky will clear, and that we will have grown because of them." Looking out at the vast water of Burrard Inlet, before Vancouver Island gives way to the Pacific Ocean, I guess I shouldn't be surprised that so many of Len's teachings come from the water.

* * *

Len shares a word from the Hunqiminum downriver dialect, which I try poorly to pronounce (as I'm guessing you also are now), uh-ee see-em chkhw muh-stay-yuh-khw (ʔi siʔém̓čxw məstéyəxw), which translates loosely as "you are a wealthy person." He explains that, for Coast Salish Peoples, wealth has little to do with possessions. We are rich because we are here now, alive to this moment in all its complexity, and able to experience it alongside others. We cannot perfectly curate the thoughts and emotions that arise within us, nor can we control everything that unfolds across a lifetime. Still, we are blessed to be present for all of it. Len is clear that some thoughts can be profoundly painful. Grief and shame, in particular, can arrive with such force that they threaten to drain hope entirely. So what can we do when those experiences surface?

As I remember it, Len explains it this way: "You can't begin a healing ceremony unless you first acknowledge who is present and what the work will be. Everybody needs to be welcomed into the lodge. It's the same with painful or intrusive thoughts. They enter the space of the heart and mind, and instead of pushing them away, we recognize them, name them, and show them respect. Even gratitude has a place there." He described this as a ceremonial way of relating to our inner lives. When we acknowledge difficult thoughts and feelings rather than resisting them, our relationship to them begins to shift. They are no longer enemies to be defeated, but experiences to be met with care. In that space, even the most distressing thoughts can be honoured for what they are trying to communicate, and eventually allowed to move through us rather than take us over.

* * *

Len shares candidly that he has struggled with doubting his own self-worth, which for some weird reason gives me a feeling of calm and relief. After all, if someone like Len Pierre has those thoughts too, maybe I'm not so weird and broken. He shares that when getting ready to speak to an audience on behalf of his community or to sit in front of a camera to share some teachings, he sometimes hears the whisper that he is not worthy and feels the power of that thought in the pit of his stomach. Rather than get in a wrestling match with the experience, Len welcomes it into his space, breathes his spirit back into the moment, remembers why he is doing the work he does, and takes the thoughts and feelings along with him for the adventure.

It is starting to get dark, and I can smell rain on its way, or perhaps this is just the smell of the West; I can't be sure. Either way, we make our way back towards Len's house, and I thank him for everything he has shared with me. On my way to the airport, my mind swirls. Have I ever welcomed painful experiences into my own space? Have I ever acknowledged them by name? Have I honoured them? I don't think so. If I am being honest, I have shouted obscenities at them, slammed the door in their faces, and nailed the windows shut. Not a very gracious host. I try to imagine approaching these experiences in the way Len describes.

"Welcome, Anxiety! I see you brought your sons, Heart Palpitations, Sweaty Palms, and Racing Thoughts. Welcome! Thanks to each of you for the warnings and for always looking to protect me from harm.

"Hello, Grief. It's been far too long, how have you been? Welcome back. I want to acknowledge your reminders of the love I have for those who have journeyed on and of my kinship responsibility to always keep them in my heart. Thank you.

"Ahh, come on in! Everyone shift over and make room for Regret and Anger. Please come sit here beside me. These two have always been here for me, letting me know when things need to change in my life. Thank you both for that."

While at first this feels like a pretty silly exercise, I notice something difficult to describe. Like a window has been opened to let a bit of cool air into a stuffy and crowded room. The difficult experiences are still with me, but in acknowledging them in this way by their names and their contributions, I feel as though my relationship with them has changed from one of conflict and resistance to one of compassion and understanding. Len might be onto something here.

"What's your anxiety's name?" Len had asked with the sun bouncing off his shades, reflecting my own distorted face back to me.

"Hmmm . . . ," I thought. "Wilma the Worrywart?" Trying to look very serious.

"Like Wilma from *The Flintstones*? Like, WIIILMAAAAA?" he yelled in his best Fred Flintstone voice. We both cracked up at this.

Sometimes, giving our experiences a name can help us relate to them with a bit more space and even a touch of humour. You might try addressing a recurring worry or a familiar critical story by a name you give it, as if greeting an old acquaintance. "Oh, there's Wilma here to warn me about all the things that might go wrong this week," or "Ah, it looks like the I'm-too-fat story is really trying to get my attention this morning!" or "Look, the *rage train* has arrived at the station right on schedule."

This way of naming acknowledges the experience in a humorous but respectful way, and reminds us that they are only a part of us, not the whole us.

I wonder what some fitting names for your difficult experiences might be?

* * *

Am I a wealthy person? Sitting in the Vancouver airport and looking over the chicken scratch of some of the notes I was able to scribble out after visiting with Len, I see my poor attempt at spelling the Coast Salish word that Len had shared with me, uh-ee see-em chkhw muh-stay-yuh-khw (which actually turned out to be ʔi siʔém̓ čxw məstéyəxw). "You are a rich person," I say to myself while chewing my pen cap beyond recognition. I can't stop thinking about Len's teaching about the meaning of wealth, that our riches include our ability to share joy and pain with others.

As I think and chew, I notice my mind doing its best to dissect Len's meaning into neat, organized pieces, to chop them up, to put them in neat little ziplock bags, and attach clean white clinical labels to each one before putting them in their appropriate place in my brain. What psychological processes are these, what diagnoses might they be appropriate for? What theory of self does this remind me of? How can this be translated for use in modern psychotherapy? I acknowledge my colonized consciousness and work hard just to listen to the teachings I've been provided.

While studying under Gros Ventre psychologist Dr. Joseph Gone at Harvard University, I once heard him ask, "Are you a lumper or a splitter?" I hadn't heard that before but started to run into it everywhere after that, like when you constantly notice a specific time on the clock or a series of numbers (9:11). The basic idea with lumpers and splitters is that human beings are prone to taking one of two approaches when looking at any phenomena. We can say, "Hey, these things are kind of similar" (lumpers), or we can say, "These things are not the same" (splitters). The same is true in research and practice across most disciplines; you have folks arguing over how things are different (splitters) or how they are the same (lumpers).

In reality, most phenomena are more complex than that; they are both similar and dissimilar simultaneously, and often it comes down to the definitions and constructs we are using that make the real comparisons or differentiations. I am doing my best to step outside of the allegiances of my professional training and my colonial education to really hear what Len has said, to see it for what it is rather than turning on the lumping-and-splitting machine in my head. It isn't easy.

Am I a wealthy person by Len's definition? Or have I hoarded my painful experiences to myself, only ever allowing people to see the side of me I want them to see? Am I curating the experiences I allow myself to have? "When was the last time I cried in front of someone else?" I think out loud before quickly dashing the thought out of my head and moving on to something else completely. I answered my own question by almost touching something too painful to manage, even in my own head. Still a ways to go.

3.

TURNING OUR HEARTS AWAY

Pain is part of being alive. Our bodies register injury. Our hearts register loss. Our minds register threat and uncertainty. These are not malfunctions. They are protective systems doing the work they evolved to do. Pulling your hand away from a hot frying pan protects you from further injury, while crying facilitates the release of endorphins and oxytocin, which reduce the intensity of your stress response. Whether physical or emotional, pain is a vital biological and psychological mechanism that alerts us to potential harm while prompting protective responses. We wouldn't survive long without the ability to perceive pain.

Suffering is about how we relate to that pain: the labels we assign to it, the reasons we give for it, what we believe the painful events say about us, and how we struggle against it. For example, losing a loved one is a naturally painful experience, and behaviours associated with emotional distress are a natural response to that loss. However, if we make certain word connections with the loss, we can intensify and prolong the painful experience indefinitely. If I believe that it is my fault that my loved one died, that I didn't do enough to keep them alive, and that makes me a bad person, I can spend years ruminating, reliving the painful experience, and never really feeling any resolution. In an effort to get some relief, I might drink alcohol or abuse prescription medications, withdraw socially and lash out at anyone or anything that is a reminder of the experience or who might affirm the painful stories my mind is generating. As the behaviours I engage in to get temporary relief from the pain begin to generate their own painful thoughts and experiences and seem to prove my "I am bad" self-story right, a vicious cycle is initiated. This is suffering.

You may have come across the saying "pain is inevitable, suffering is optional." I think that makes a lot of sense. Psychological suffering could be described as the distress that arises from our efforts to evade painful experiences. By understanding the dynamic interplay between pain, language, and cognition, we can navigate our experiences with greater clarity, minimize unnecessary suffering, and turn our focus to the things we truly want our lives to be about. But again, this is often easier said than done. On my own healing journey, I found two ideas from contextual behavioural science that helped me put words to this experience: experiential avoidance and psychological flexibility.

Experiential avoidance is a term often used to describe our instinctive attempts to eliminate unwanted thoughts, feelings, and sensations or to control our experiences in order to get some relief and feel better. Unfortunately, these efforts often backfire in the long run, exacerbating our suffering instead of alleviating it. This likely stems from our natural inclination to solve problems in a logical and sequential manner, a practice that has proven extremely useful when confronting external challenges like a flat tire or a leaky roof. However, when we apply this analytical problem-solving approach to our internal struggles, it is sometimes more harmful than helpful. In fact, experiential avoidance may be at the core of many forms of psychological suffering we label mental illness.

Our efforts to eradicate anxiety, depression, painful memories, and unwanted thoughts and sensations often lead to behaviours that bring short-term relief while carrying longer-term costs. The urge to fix what hurts is compelling, especially when relief appears to follow, even briefly. Paradoxically, when we come to see our experiences as problems in need of a solution, our very attempts to find a remedy become the source of the problem itself. The mind shifts into fixing mode, treating inner experience as something to be controlled or eliminated rather than understood.

This orientation is reinforced by the cultural environment we inhabit. Our desire to turn our problem-solving machinery inward is met by an entire economy organized around self-improvement and happiness. The market for drugs, alcohol, diets, fitness equipment, self-improvement courses, coaching, therapies, social media gurus, and beauty products repeatedly delivers the same message: You are broken and need to be fixed. We are bombarded daily with messages touting the merits of experiential avoidance ("positive vibes only," "don't worry, be happy"). Over time, these patterns of fixing can narrow our lives, pulling attention away from what matters and amplifying the very suffering we are trying to escape.

Although I've painted a fairly grim picture, and your mind may already be spinning off into dark associations, it's important to say this clearly: Experiential avoidance is not inherently bad or wrong. In many situations, it is both protective and necessary. Pulling your hand away from an aggressive dog or leaving an abusive relationship are forms of avoidance that can quite literally save a life. Taking a painkiller for a headache or slowing your breathing before a medical procedure can also be skilful ways of managing discomfort so that you can do what matters in the moment.

Experiential avoidance only becomes problematic when it

begins to shrink our lives rather than grow them. This often happens gradually and without much notice. For example, when anxiety shows up, a person may start organizing their day around keeping that feeling at bay. That might mean steering clear of certain people or places, while also spending a great deal of mental energy trying to distract themselves, argue with anxious thoughts, or manage inner sensations. I used to count things or make lists in my head to keep the feeling from taking over.

At first, these strategies can bring some relief. Over time, though, they can consume large portions of a day and limit access to things that actually matter. Before long, I might find myself alone, lost in my thoughts and efforts to stay regulated, instead of being outside, listening to music, making art, or spending time with my family. That kind of life might feel safer, but it is far from vibrant, meaningful, or alive. Is there another way?

Psychological flexibility is often used to describe a person's capacity to respond to situations in ways that support what they care about, even when thoughts, emotions, or bodily reactions are difficult or unpleasant. When we are psychologically flexible, we have a curious and compassionate relationship with our thoughts and emotions, while also taking purposeful action in the direction of a rich and meaningful life. It emphasizes a willingness to stay in relationship with experience, even when it is uncomfortable, and to make choices that align with what matters most.

In contrast to experiential avoidance of anxiety, psychological flexibility involves staying engaged with the situation as it unfolds, even when anxiety and the thoughts and sensations that accompany it are present, rather than organizing our behaviour around trying to make those experiences stop. Importantly, this doesn't mean liking the experience at all. I don't know anyone who would enjoy having a panic attack or feeling very depressed. A psychologically flexible response also isn't about merely tolerating or enduring distress. Many of us fall into a grin-and-bear-it strategy, living what have been called "lives of quiet desperation." We clench everything and battle the experience head-on. While this might allow us to get through a painful moment, such as a root canal, few of us would want to spend the rest of our lives in the dentist's chair.

When I encounter terms like *psychological flexibility*, my first question is always about what that actually looks like. Exactly how does someone "do" psychological flexibility? What actions can I actually take to walk in this way?

I think it starts with noticing. Is the behaviour I'm engaging in, at this moment, aimed at finding relief from something uncomfortable, or is it an action that brings me closer to what matters most in my heart? Am I making the zombie trip to the fridge and peeking inside to get away from boredom or sadness? Am I calling a friend to get some relief from guilt or the thought that they might be mad at me? Am I going to the gym to outrun some self-critical thought? Am I getting a glass of water because wellness is important to me? Am I doing a load of laundry because sharing responsibilities in my relationship is important? Am I taking the kids to a new park because being a caring and attentive parent matters?

There's a pattern that shows up when we start to look closely. When I'm preoccupied by an old story, a painful thought, an uncomfortable tension in my chest, I often go for things that offer short-term relief. And the kick in the teeth is that these things work just enough in the moment that they become very easy to repeat. But when I zoom out and look at the day or week as a whole, I can see the loop, and I can see those difficult experiences intensifying rather than going away. When I pause and notice these attempts to get some relief from difficult experiences, though, even just for a few seconds, I can sometimes do something different. Every now and then, when I'm engaging in behaviour that might get me sucked into that familiar cycle of reacting quickly to discomfort and reaching for relief, I pause and notice. Sometimes I ask myself what it might look like to let this moment be guided by what matters most to me, even with the discomfort sitting there. That question alone can give me a little more room to breathe and a bit more freedom to choose.

* * *

"But do I have to like it?" An important note here, from my own early misunderstanding of healing. A flexible stance doesn't mean accepting, agreeing with, justifying, or validating the source of our difficult experiences. I am typically not a fan of the word *acceptance*, because it seems to suggest that we should be okay with the things that have happened to us; just get over it, right?

While this might be reasonable if we are talking about the anger I have upon finding another little scratch on my truck, it is a whole other thing if we are talking about a history of sexual abuse or the violent death of a loved one. There are few scenarios where the word *acceptance* is going to go over well with people who have experienced such unspeakable trauma.

I much prefer the word *willingness.*

As in a willingness to sit with an experience as it is. A willingness to make room for what your heart, body, mind, and spirit are telling you. A willingness to be kind to yourself while going through this difficult time. A willingness to choose what matters most in your life, even when it hurts.

Grandmother Renée shared a teaching about a tree in the wind that has been burned into my memory: "The tree takes the full brunt of the weather and never complains. It welcomes the wind and rain with open arms. If you don't bend like that, you're going to break." When I hear those words, I hear a reminder about what it takes to stay standing in a world that does not pause for us. We don't want to stop the wind or shelter ourselves from the rain and snow forever. The tree needs the wind and the rain to be healthy. It needs the winter to cleanse itself of pests and disease and to recycle vital nutrients. If we are able to move with the wind and feel the rain on our leaves and the snow at our roots, they can make us strong. In fact, without these things, we may not survive.

While speaking with Grandmother Renée and Len (and the other Knowledge Keepers you will meet along the way), I was struck by their ability to explain these complex constructs in such an accessible way. Neither of them had ever heard of contextual behavioural science, RFT, or ACT, yet they explained concepts like experiential avoidance and psychological flexibility more clearly than any expert trainer I've encountered so far.

In our sharing circle, Dr. Hayes said that the science of psychological flexibility is just now arriving where the ancient knowledge traditions have been all along (I know I'm repeating myself, but it's worth repeating). These concepts are not new and are likely to be found in some shape or form in the healing practices of cultures the world over. That said, they are far from common sense.

Many of us (definitely me included) have spent an incredible amount of time, money, and energy at war with our difficult experiences, doing everything we can think of to rid ourselves of anxiety, fear, anger, and grief, often with detrimental outcomes in our relationships and more of those yucky experiences we were trying to get rid of in the first place. If you make a list of the things you have done to "fix yourself" or to get rid of difficult experiences, you'll likely find that it quickly becomes a very long list. You'll also probably find that few if any of these strategies have accomplished the goal of forever banishing those difficult thoughts, memories, or sensations. How might we learn to bend with the wind instead?

One of the ways I have started to learn to bend is to get a bit of distance from the difficult experiences, while still remaining in contact with them. Most of the time we don't perceive of our thoughts as thoughts, we just experience them as us. That voice in my head commenting on how chunky I've got while I brush my teeth in the morning is me, isn't it? No, it's not. I am not the voice in my head, and I am not the heaviness in my chest. I don't think that my liver, kidneys, ankle, or teeth are me. I wouldn't say, "I am sore ankle today," or "Ouch! I am toothache," but we instantly give such credit to our thoughts and emotions; they are us, we *are* angry, I *am* depressed. Our thoughts are so ever-present that we give our mind the privilege of defining our identity completely. We become those thoughts and feelings. So of course they are absolutely true and the most important thing going on, right?

But what if I am not my thoughts, feelings, memories, or sensations? What if those are just things that I have? Things that I hold? What if they are parts of me that are important, but they aren't all of me? What if I am more? What if, instead, I am a whole being with a physical body and an emotional self, cognitive abilities and a spirit? What if I am a part of the world around me in an intimate and inseparable way? Things start to look a bit different when we notice our thoughts as thoughts and our feelings as feelings. In an interpersonal conflict, "I am having the thought that he's being disrespectful, and I am feeling a tension in my shoulders and a lump growing in my throat" is very different from "I am angry and I don't take no crap from no one!"

When you find yourself wrestling with a difficult experience, or when you are walking alongside someone who is, carrying a few gentle questions in your heart can be a powerful way to get some distance without escaping your experience. Instead of searching for immediate answers or solutions, you might simply create a space for inquiry. You could gently ask yourself, or invite the person you are supporting to wonder, What is my mind telling me right now, and how is it urging me to react? Turning inward, what is my heart sharing, and can I listen to it with kindness? Where do I feel this experience in my body, and what happens if I just sit with it for a moment, allowing it to be as it naturally is? What might this experience truly need from me, and how could I respond with patience and self-compassion in this moment? Is there room to hold this thought, this feeling, this sensation, gently? Is there a part of me that is being ignored in the presence of this experience, and can I bring my mind, body, heart, and spirit together in this moment? How might I honour this experience as a part of my journey, a teacher perhaps, rather than something to be fixed or avoided? If I allow myself to fully feel this, what new understanding, what quiet wisdom, might emerge? These sorts of questions give us an opportunity to notice our tendency towards experiential avoidance and to take a psychologically flexible stance instead.

Len's perspective on pain and suffering provides us with an important teaching on getting some distance from our experiences. Len mentioned "being in relationship with anxiety" and "visiting with depression." Eduardo Duran, a psychologist from the Apache and Tewa Nations, suggested something similar in his soul wound psychology, which focuses on the collective harm of colonization and advocates for cultural reconnection, traditional healing practices, and spiritual revitalization as vital components of the healing process. Duran frames the struggle with alcohol as receiving a visit from the spirit of alcohol, or depression as receiving a visit from the spirit of depression. As many Indigenous worldviews and language systems position all things as containing spirit, this way of talking about mental health challenges may be a familiar way to separate ourselves from our experiences.

I had a close encounter with the spirit of my suffering once. Dr. Kelly Wilson, the rock-star-looking psychologist I mentioned earlier, was in town doing a two-day session. It must have been around 2010. By that point I had been to dozens of workshops and conferences on all sorts of therapies and strategies, and I was expecting the usual. Worn hotel carpets. Aluminum padded chairs, always in some strange pattern. Cups of mediocre, lukewarm coffee. Wraps and sandwiches for lunch.

I did not expect to be shaken to my core that day.

After a very brief introduction, Kelly moved into an experiential activity. Like many people, I hate the part where someone says, "Okay, now close your eyes," or "Grab a partner." I had given serious thought to bailing to the bathroom or heading out for some fresh air when I realized it would be one of those workshops. I stayed. I closed my eyes. I tried to get comfortable in the ninety-degree posture chairs, surrounded by the breath and shifting of about a hundred people around me.

Then came Kelly's voice over the PA.

If you have not heard Kelly speak, it is difficult to describe. He speaks without polish or performance. Warm. Soft. Somehow intense and powerful at the same time. You can tell there is a brilliant scientist in there, but the person who takes the floor is a human being.

After a few breaths, I noticed my shoulders drop. I almost forgot about the strange room I was in as Kelly's voice pulled my attention inward.

A familiar thought floated to the front of my mind. A painful one that had been with me for as long as I could remember. That I was wrong. Bad. Evil, even. That I hurt people. That I deserved every difficulty I had encountered in my life and more. That I was destined to suffer. That things would only get worse. That everyone would eventually see the real me and be repulsed. That I would be punished. That others were angry with me. That others were trying to hurt me.

My mind raced, stacking these thoughts higher and higher, layering them with adjectives, rationales, and supporting arguments, until Kelly's voice broke through again.

Somehow, I had already forgotten where I was. I was in a conference room in a hotel in downtown Toronto. It felt like I had been gone for a long time. Time no longer worked the same way.

Then I saw it.

That thought and feeling had condensed into a single experience. All those words collapsed into one phrase.

You are hated.

At first, I saw the letters spelled out in my mind, rendered in a metallic block font that looked like it would be cold to the touch. As I watched, the letters curled together and folded in on themselves, taking on a viscous quality, like mercury or molten steel. Jet-black. Hollow. Heavy.

The surface of this thought took on a rough, almost ugly quality, like those strange fruits you see in the grocery store but are too wary to buy. It was hard and sharp and very cold. As I watched it shimmer and shift, I realized I was seeing it inside my body, as if I were looking down into my stomach with some kind of X-ray vision.

There it was, sitting where my ribs meet above my diaphragm. The solar plexus, I think it is called.

I was startled by this and felt a sinking, nauseous sensation as it moved. I watched from this strange observatory as black, thorny vines began to sprout from it, like a potato left too long in the cupboard. They searched outward, looking for something solid. One vine wrapped around each lung, and my breath grew shallow. I tried to pull more air in, but it felt as though someone was squeezing me too tightly.

Another vine crept up my back, over my shoulders, up the back of my neck, knotting itself around my brainstem and sending an electric tingle from my ears downwards. Two more tendrils spread across my chest and down into the palms of my hands, which began to feel clammy.

My mind did what it always does. It tried to flee from the image and the sensations that came with it. Kelly's voice pulled me back again, asking me to stay with something that I now realized had been there for a very long time.

With disgust, surprise, anxiety, and horror, I watched as this black entity spread through my nervous system. It grew larger in my chest, pushing aside my heart and lungs, taking up too much space, choking my breath. I think I let out a strange sound, a kind of silent scream that I disguised as a cough or clearing of my throat. For a brief moment I remembered where I was; then I was pulled back again.

I would have given anything to be free of it in that moment.

The mass grew eyes. Square pupils, like those of a goat, impossible to read, giving it a dull, all-seeing quality that followed without moving. Then came a mouth, a small opening at the centre, lined with rows of fine needle teeth like a jackfish. As it worked, it sent small shocks through my body, stealing my breath and making my heart skip, my vision fading in and out.

It did not seem bothered by being watched. It carried on with its task, indifferent to me in my observer's box.

Then Kelly's voice returned again, calling the creature forward with a hypnotic steadiness. To my surprise, it responded. It floated out of my chest, its jagged tendrils still threaded through my body.

I could see it now, hovering just above the banquet table, between my coffee cup and the steel water jug at the centre. For a moment, we watched each other in silence.

What do you need from me? I asked silently.

There was a long pause. No response.

I asked again.

What do you need from me?

Its eyes met mine somehow, and without sound or words it answered.

I need you to keep me alive.

I need you to hear me.

I need you to see and feel me.

I need us to be safe together.

I took a breath, and the tendrils shifted on my lungs and heart. They did not release, but they loosened enough to let air move again.

I nodded.

Reaching into my pocket, I pulled out a small, round stone, grey with a white stripe running cleanly through the centre, the kind you always pick up and keep when you find it in a river. I looked at it, then extended my hand.

A black tendril reached out and wrapped around the stone, drawing it close. The square eyes blinked, perhaps in gratitude.

When I guided the creature back into my body, it felt cold, but lighter.

I see you, I said.

TRAPLINES AND TIME TRAVEL, PART 2

"Mósom?" I ask as I set down two buckets of water hauled up from down the bank.

"Yes, my boy?" my grandfather says. He's cleaning fish again, but these ones are suckers. He dips one in the first bucket I set down to get some of the slime off. His hands move slow and sure. He presses his thumb against the backbone and draws the blade in a steady line, keeping close to the bones. He flips the fillet, runs the knife under the skin, and, pinning it down at the edge with his fingernails, pulls it clean in one long strip.

"Do you feel pain where you are now?" My eyes are fixed on the growing pile of fillets on the piece of cardboard.

"Oh, not for a long time, my boy. Don't need it anymore," he says with a small smile. "You might not believe me, but you might just miss it someday."

I think on this and find it hard to imagine ever missing grief, anxiety, or loneliness. "I've thought about your question, Mósom," I say, handing him the next fish from the black tub.

"Oh?" I watch him rinse the blade in the other pail before setting it to the next spine. The water is red now.

"Maybe pain is a visitor whose message is always about what

we love. It's a fluid current, an intimate part of being alive. It's a teacher, Mósom, though sometimes a tough and even chaotic one. It's our spirit's protective alarm bell, our crap detector, our body's honest truth. It's a heavy blessing and a sacred gift. It's a storm that makes our roots grow deep."

"Mmm-hmm," he says again. He managed to get through another fish while I stumbled through all that. He looks up and gives me a soft smile, then points with his lips to the second bucket of water. I wake up as I set it down beside him.

THE POWER OF METAPHOR

You may have noticed that Len and Grandmother Renée's teachings paint a picture in your mind as you hear them. Whether we are pulling the reins on a wild stallion or lugging our collection of rocks up the mountain trail, there is a deeper sense of meaning and connection when the teachings are shared in this way.

Throughout this learning journey, I found each of the Knowledge Keepers to possess this skill, to speak in pictures and to create expansive relationships in the concepts they spoke to. Metaphor can be a powerful tool in building psychological flexibility. Many of our problems of experiential avoidance are rooted in inflexible associations. We hear our partner say they wish we'd be more helpful around the house, and we build a one-way route to our inadequacies and their vindictiveness. After a while this route can become pretty well-worn, making it easier and quicker to jump to the more we practise it. Before long, a request for help becomes a story about our uselessness, and only that. And so, we respond in a defensive and rigid way, failing to see all the other possible relationships that might exist in such a request. We could see the request as a sign that we are part of a team or that we are important and needed. But due to long histories of using our problem-solving brains to rid ourselves of uncomfortable stimuli, we tend to go down route one first.

Metaphors have the quality of forming many relationships quickly. If my thoughts are a stampede of wild stallions, and I am grabbing on to the reins, suddenly there are qualities of the experience (fast, strong, wild, free, challenging, exciting, powerful) that weren't there before, and I am able to step back from my usual connections, pause, and consider the usefulness of my repertoire of rigid responding. If my thoughts are stampeding wild stallions, it is much easier for me to see them as something I have, rather than something I am. If my thoughts are painted rocks in my backpack, then they are clearly not me, and I am not obliged to do what they say.

Metaphors create a richer perceptual experience that is more memorable than the simple descriptive syntax often found in treatment manuals. You may forget many of the technical explanations you've read so far in this chapter, like the technical definitions of experiential avoidance or psychological flexibility, but you are likely to remember that tree bending in the wind, the nutrients we can obtain as we digest our difficult experiences, and the troubling thought turned three-eyed purple creature pressing low beneath your ribs.

When I notice myself struggling, the first thoughts that tend to show up are blunt and rigid. "It's terrible. I hate this. This shouldn't be happening. I can't handle this." That kind of language arrives quickly for me, often before I have much say in the matter. I do not always catch it, but when I do, when I can take a breath, notice my feet on the ground, or look around the room with all five senses, I sometimes see those statements as thoughts rather than facts, and a small amount of space opens up. From there, I can ask, "What is this like for me?" The first answer that my mind comes up with is rarely polished. It is still rough, but it is more descriptive. *Heavy. Tight. Pressing.* When I stay with that for a moment longer, I can ask again, "What is that like for me?" Each time I am able to slow down and ask, the picture sharpens. The experience begins to take form. A stack of bricks on my chest. A cave with the walls closing in. A fire burning low and steady in my body. With each pass, the description carries more detail and less and less judgment. The picture grows richer, and I am able to notice what is happening without needing to escape it.

CULTURE AS MEDICINE

Again, these ways of being are hardly new; Indigenous peoples around the world have nurtured a stance of willingness in the very structure of our languages, in our ceremonies, songs, stories, and helping practices for countless generations. Drawing upon these cultural tools can be a powerful current in our healing, helping us make room for all that life brings while walking in the direction of a life of meaning and vitality. While sacred knowledge and Ceremony are best sought in relationship with Elders and Knowledge Keepers, many of our day-to-day cultural practices offer paths for personal connection and for developing our ability to meet life with an open heart.

For instance, if you are a language keeper or have a relationship with one, you might explore how an experience you have been wrestling with would be described in the language of your ancestors. What are the words for loneliness or heartbreak or even for that deep well of anxiety? How are these words built, what worlds of meaning do their morphemes open up, and what relationships do they reveal? This exploration itself can be a powerful way to cultivate flexibility in how we see our inner lives.

Our traditions also remind us that the land is our best therapist and is there for us 24/7. Spending time in the outside air—among the trees, birds, sun, and sky—offers a natural context for sitting with whatever you are carrying. You might sit by the water and imagine each thought floating by on its own lily pad, or place a difficult feeling on a falling leaf and just watch it with gentle attention. You could even imagine the sensations in your body having a counterpart in the trunk and branches of a nearby tree. The land has a way of opening us to the natural flow of being a spirit on a human journey.

There is power in storying and restorying our experiences. Our stories are the lifeblood of our cultures, carrying teachings about our relationships with ourselves and with Creation itself. I often think back to the adventures of Wīsahkēcāhk, the trickster hero from Cree stories; laughing by the fire as a boy, I was unknowingly receiving lessons on living a good life.

Storytelling offers a way to meet our difficult experiences with willingness and curiosity. As we explored with the spirit of suffering, we can personify an experience, give it a name, or visualize it as a character. Then we can begin to tell its story: Where did it come from? Where might it be going? What are its adventures, its challenges, its allies? We can also tell the story of our own journey, seeing our experiences as vital plot points, challenges, and moments of growth for ourselves as the protagonists. If a heartache feels like the whole story, remembering it is just one part of the story can open up space for more to be written.

BRINGING IT HOME

In this first part of the journey, we explored the concept of psychological flexibility enhanced by the helping wisdom offered by Grandmother Renée and Len Pierre. Through their teachings, the significance of otōtīmowin, a relational way of being, a stance that allows us to willingly engage with life's challenges and joys without being trapped in rigid patterns of behaviour, becomes clear.

Experiential avoidance, while useful in protecting us from harm, can become a stumbling block to leading a life of vitality and fulfillment when it becomes the focal point of our journeys and our primary tool for interacting with our world. Cultivating psychological flexibility offers us an alternative: the ability to respond adaptively to the present moment, embracing discomfort and distressing experiences while taking purposeful actions aligned with our values and goals. It urges us to develop a compassionate relationship with our thoughts, emotions, memories, and sensations so that we can make choices that enrich our lives rather than shrink them.

Drawing upon our languages and helping practices provides culturally relevant ways to cultivate psychological flexibility, ways that have kept our people healthy for generations upon generations. Remember, this journey is uniquely yours. There's no one-size-fits-all approach to making space for our pain. Pay attention to how you respond to discomfort in the coming days. Can you create a bit more space for your experiences, even the difficult ones? How might you be willing to learn, grow, and seek balance as your life continues to change? I am grateful that you have walked with me this far and am excited to see where our travels take us next. There's much more to explore.

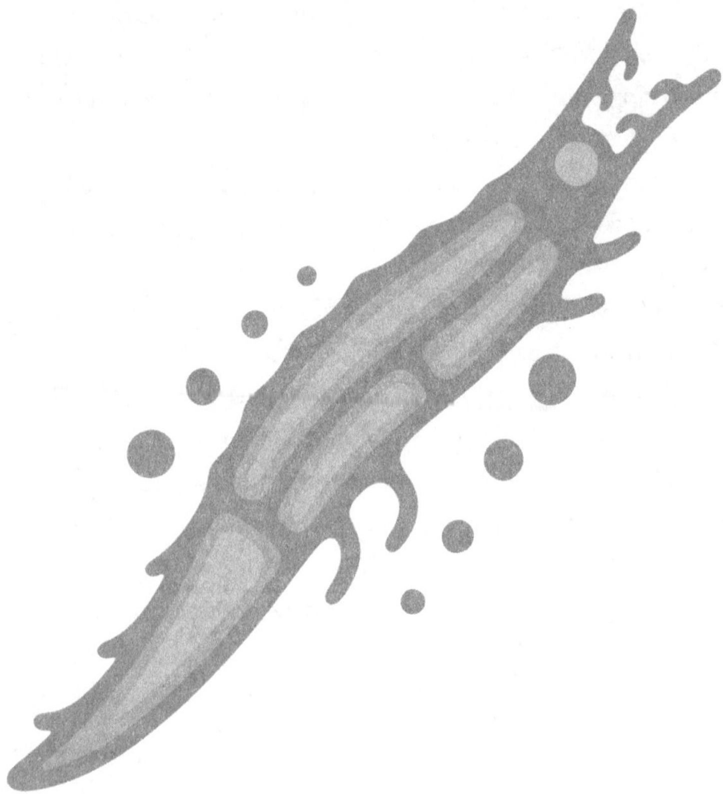

ĀKĀWĀMISOWIN

Our thoughts, physical sensations, emotions, dreams, and our words are inseparably connected to the earth and to the stars. Each part of us has been weaved into the ecological fabric of the universe. When we forget this, the natural order of things is disturbed, and we struggle.

Bomgiizhik (Isaac Murdoch)

4.

ĀKĀWĀMISOWIN

The Cree word *ākāwāmisowin* carries a teaching about being fully present in the world. It speaks to a way of moving that is alert, careful, and rooted in relationship. The word comes from *ākā*, which refers to attentiveness, and *wāmiso*, which speaks to looking after oneself. The suffix *-win* shapes it into a state of being. Together, ākāwāmisowin expresses a quality of presence that is both internal and external—a practice of looking after ourselves by paying close attention to the conditions around us, the state of our inner world, and the needs that emerge moment by moment.

In seeking a fuller understanding of this term, Simon Bird consulted Elder Roger Ratt, a th-dialect Cree speaker and member of the Lac La Ronge Indian Band. Roger is a deeply respected Elder and Knowledge Keeper and an important resource for older words and teachings such as this one. He described ākāwāmisowin through the image of a person walking on newly frozen ice. When the ice is only six inches thick, and the water beneath is dark and moving, each step must be deliberate. The walker carries a stick, not from fear, but from readiness. They listen. They look. They tap the ice in front of them with care. This is the wisdom to move slowly, to read the signs offered by the world around us, and to bring ourselves fully into the moment to get where we are going.

In this context, ākāwāmisowin becomes a guide for how we relate to our own minds, bodies, and spirits. We walk this way when we recognize that each experience holds meaning. It is the posture of someone who walks carefully through shifting inner terrain. It is the practice of listening inward and outward at the same time. Which isn't easy.

This way of being turns us towards the present. It is to be in relationship with our surroundings while staying in touch with the stirrings of our inner life. This may mean noticing the way tension settles in the shoulders before a hard conversation. It may mean recognizing the breath quicken as a memory surfaces. It may mean hearing a critical thought and choosing to pause and be curious about it before acting. Each moment is a thread that can pull towards connection.

Akāwamisowin also involves looking after oneself with intention. This includes caring for the physical body, but also tending to the needs of the heart, the mind, and the spirit. It is a teaching of balance. It reminds us that wellness is a result of daily choices that honour who we are and the pain that we carry.

This way of being means tapping into an expansive understanding of our true selves. Beyond our "I am" stories, there is an unbreakable, unchanging spiritual part of us that exists. Again, it isn't easy. Developing presence is like working out; with persistence, we become stronger, more flexible, and more agile. Those who have embraced spiritual practices such as fasting, prayer, or meditation over long periods of time may have a deeper familiarity with this sense of present-moment awareness. For many of us, this will likely take some practice. But I'm certain that if my very distractible mind can find the present moment every once in a while, then yours can too.

Where and who are we? Have you ever found yourself physically present but mentally miles away? Maybe you've driven somewhere, and upon arriving you realize that you have no recollection of actually driving there. Or while someone is speaking, you stop listening because your mind is jumping to a solution for their problem, or your mind has found a similar story to share and is fully focused on that instead of the person you're with? Me too.

Our minds have a habit of spacing out and time-travelling instead of hanging out here in the present. In an instant we get sucked into the past, ruminating about this mistake we made or that thing someone said that hurt us. The next instant we are transported to the future, imagining the idealized life we'll have when things finally start to go our way, or dreading a future where things might go terribly, horribly wrong. When our minds time-travel, there's a good chance we are missing what's happening and what is possible right here, right now.

To make things even more challenging, while we are travelling back and forth from past to future, our minds are busy building all kinds of stories about us. You are probably familiar with some of the stories you carry about yourself. They usually start with "I am" and are followed by some description, rule, or judgment: I am anxious, I am strong-willed, I am a loser, I am a leader, I am fat, I am proud, I am unlovable. The list goes on and on as our minds turn the association-generating game inward.

The problem with these stories, whether we might label them as good or bad, mean or nice, is that they can restrict our ability to respond to our world in a flexible way. If I am anxious, there are things I cannot or should not do. An anxious person doesn't speak up at a meeting, an anxious person doesn't go to the party, an anxious person doesn't introduce themselves to someone at the social. Likewise, a strong-willed person never shows weakness, never gives up even when something is harming them, doesn't seek validation from others, doesn't settle for anything but perfection. It's easy to see how the stories we carry, good or bad, mean or nice, can start to shrink our worlds and give us fewer and fewer options on how to interpret and respond to our experiences.

On our walk out on the West Coast, Len had commented on how easily the mind slips away from the present moment, and about our tendency to drift backward into old stories or forward into worry, and how that movement often pulls us out of balance. "We can get stuck on what happened ten minutes ago, ten hours ago, or ten years ago." When that happens, he said, we are no longer fully here. The body may still be moving through the present, but the mind has already left, caught up in what was or what might be. Worry about bills, concern for someone who is ill, or anticipation of what lies ahead can draw us just as far away as rumination about the past.

Len framed these tendencies not as a personal failure, but as another natural part of being human. What matters is how we find our way back. He shared some of the cultural practices of the Coast Salish Peoples that are meant to call the travelling spirit home again. Prayer, in particular, came up as a way of returning attention to the present. Prayer is rooted in gratitude. It is a way of acknowledging Creation and giving thanks for what is already here. When that appreciation is felt, he said, our minds can settle. We become more connected to ourselves and to the world around us. From that place, the present moment feels accessible, and we can meet our day with a sense of openness. He emphasized that this is a practice rather than a destination. We are unlikely to get it right once and for all. It is something we return to, again and again, especially when life becomes demanding.

In the pages ahead, we will continue to learn from those who carry this teaching in their way of being. Through their words, and through your own reflections, you may come to know what ākāwāmisowin feels like in your own body, mind, heart, and spirit. Let's get back on the road and see what else we can learn.

5.

BOMGIIZHIK (ISAAC MURDOCH)

The next visit on our journey brings us to Nimkii Aazhibikoong, a culture camp deep in the woods on the north shore of Lake Huron. Here we find Isaac Murdoch, also known as Bomgiizhik of the Great Lakes by the many learners who listen to his stories and teachings each night. Isaac is a Fish Clan member of Serpent River First Nation, a gifted artist, musician, storyteller, environmentalist, activist, and ceremonial conductor, but these words don't really capture the entity that is Isaac Murdoch.

He is a force of nature who is constantly in some act of relationship-building and creative design, whether it be chopping wood for the new lodge he is building for a youth retreat or painting a mural on the pavement of Wall Street in New York City in protest of extractive industries. Nimkii Aazhibikoong is a testament to Isaac's vision, as he is one of the founders of the camp that offers language immersion, land-based living and learning programs, storytelling, and Ceremony.

As we sit by the fire, sipping strong percolated coffee, I am struck by the amount of knowledge that Isaac's head holds. He is a fountain of information on art, music, history, the Ojibwe language, ancient pictographs, politics, and bushcraft. He also carries what seems like an infinite number of stories, which have been passed down to him through the oral tradition. Most striking of all, however, are Isaac's insights into the human condition, into the nature of suffering, and about the path of the good life.

Isaac's own life is an incredible story on the capacity of human beings to heal after immense hardship. Isaac grew up in the bush with his family, living off the land until he and his siblings were apprehended by Indian agents and forced onto the reserve. Isaac's mother died shortly after her children were taken from her. Like many First Nations Peoples on Turtle Island, Isaac has lost many family members to violence, overdose, and suicide. Isaac is open about his experience as a survivor of childhood sexual abuse and shares his story to encourage men with similar experiences to seek help. And in what I can only imagine is the most painful experience a human being can have on this earth, Isaac tragically lost two children in an accident.

By any measure, Isaac should be a broken and bitter man. But the opposite is true. He glows and seems to peer into your soul with a sort of kindness that makes you feel instantly among family in his company. His laugh is contagious, and his message is consistently one of kindness and connection. I was very motivated to learn whatever I could from Isaac and honoured to be able to spend time hearing some of his teachings.

I tell Isaac about the learning journey I am on and my hopes of bringing Indigenous helping wisdom and the science of psychological flexibility together in a way that each may benefit from the other. Isaac reflects on the word *acceptance* and shares, "There is an inherent part of us that accepts the difficult situations we encounter in this life, but our minds like to fight back and construct all sorts of explanations as a way to escape having to face the pain of a difficult experience like loss, betrayal, or failure." Isaac repeats the word *daapnaan*, which he describes as the Ojibwe version of "it is what it is." He says daapnaan speaks to accepting something, letting the situation be as it is, whether it is an outcome, a feeling, or a dream, even if it is extremely painful. Isaac says our experience here on earth is a process of spiritual training, and that all the experiences we have, especially the difficult and chaotic ones, are like a higher learning curriculum for our spirit and for the future.

Isaac insists that pain and suffering have always been crucial in Indigenous healing philosophies, reflecting a deep understanding that mental health and spiritual health are tightly intertwined. He says that at the core of the struggle, especially in cases as extreme as suicide, it isn't just a mental health problem, but a disconnection from one's spirit, the essence that binds us to our true selves and the universe.

"Since the time of our Creation Story," Isaac continues, "pain and suffering have been seen as gifts in Ceremony," offering a pathway to healing through acknowledging and embracing our innermost struggles and reconnecting with spirit. Isaac points to fasting and offerings that occur within the ceremonies of some nations on Turtle Island. The experience of pain is offered to the Spirits, Isaac says, in order to facilitate healing in ourselves, our families, and our communities. In Ceremony, suffering is viewed as a privilege and an opportunity.

Growing up, the old ones would say, "Oh, you received a blessing!" when you got hurt, Isaac shares. He recalls being puzzled at his grandparents saying, "Hey, that's a blessing!" when he burned his finger in the fire once. "That's what they'd say when you burned yourself or got cut! You got a blessing!" Isaac says with an expression of disbelief at his own words. Now he realizes this was a powerful teaching about the nature of suffering. "Offering your pain as a trade for healing is a great honour," Isaac says. This willingness to feel something unpleasant does something important to one's view on the meaning of pain.

Hearing Isaac's teaching, I recall the third day of fasting during my first Sun Dance. I was feeling particularly miserable and sorry for myself. One of the other dancers had just quit. I was tired, hungry, thirsty, and starting to think quitting might not be such a bad idea, when an old man came up to me and said, "Thank you for your sacrifice; your ancestors are proud of you." Of course I started ugly crying.

Just that short sentence changed my perspective in that moment drastically. Suddenly all the relationships I had been building with my pain were flipped on their heads. Where once there was only "bad, hurt, tired, sad, ouch, stop, quit, escape," there was also now "gratitude, opportunity, ancestors, pride, belonging." I have said it before, and I'll say it again: More things can be accomplished in a four-day ceremony on the land than can be accomplished in a year of psychotherapy. This was certainly one of those experiences for me.

Speak to your mind. "Our mind is its own entity," Isaac says. "It's hardwired in a certain way, and whether it is due to our traumas or some hereditary thing passed down to us, we can become prone to evaluating the things around us as constant crises, and we can ascribe stories to ourselves to explain these crises. Why does this keep happening to me? I'm so stupid, I deserve this." I ask Isaac about his perspective on the tendency of our mind to work against us when things get difficult. Why kick us when we are down? Isaac shares that Medicine People would sometimes work on someone struggling with an emotional, spiritual, or mental experience by laying that person down, offering tobacco, and speaking directly to the person's mind. The Medicine Person would ask the mind to be kind to that person, would give gratitude for all that it was doing to protect the person, but would petition the mind to allow the individual to continue to live their life in a good way.

If I think about someone wise speaking to my troubled mind, it is my dad. I can picture him sitting there, calm, steady, and unhurried (probably smoking a cigar). Maybe he'd put his hand on my forehead and just sit silently for a while. He is both a man of few words and a powerful orator. Every time I've seen him get up to speak, be it a celebration, a conference, or a funeral, I am always awestruck by how easily he has the unflinching attention of the room. In that space, sitting with my mind, I think he would probably pray, and if he spoke to my mind, he might say something like "Hey, Mind, I see you're bringing warnings and worries. That's your job. We'll take those with us and take the next step," or maybe "Mind, you can be worried, but you don't have to fix anything right now."

I think about how those words would land, and how different they would be from the usual way I talk to my mind. Who would you choose to speak to your mind? What would they say if they were right there with you?

Isaac points out that Indigenous cultures have always embraced the present moment. "It's the only way to be successful at living in small communities and hacking life out in the bush," he says. "There just isn't room for ruminating on the past or living for some distant future, when you're fighting to survive and living in close quarters with your entire extended family!"

Being mindful and being present have also always been an integral part of Anishinaabe Ceremony. Isaac shares the story of his first experience alone out on the land. He was very young and out on a long walk in the bush with his grandfather. His grandfather told him to sit and listen to the trees, to hear them talk to each other, and then he left and didn't return until the next morning. Isaac admits he was frightened, but he also remembers growing intensely aware of his own body, the world around him, and the relationship between the two while he sat there in Creation.

A few years later, Isaac would go on his first vision quest, an extended period of isolation and fasting on the land at a sacred place, where he would experience an intense sense of presence and connection and receive important guidance on his life path. More than just an opportunity for meditation and internal reflection, these ceremonies help us connect to what is tangible, to what is here outside of our bodies, to what is real. Isaac recalls watching the clouds, listening to trees, feeling rocks and grass under his feet, carefully breathing the cool night air, and seeing the sun come up as it had never before. To Isaac, this process of cultivating presence and interconnectivity is crucial to moving forward in life in a good way.

Isaac shares the Ojibwe word *maapii*, which translates to something like "right here." It isn't just used to refer to a physical location, however; it also signifies a point in time, so something like "right here, right now" would probably be a closer representation of the word's meaning. Isaac says the word is foundational in the Ojibwe language and is found everywhere, in song and Ceremony and in day-to-day usage.

He adds the caveat that even "right here, right now" probably isn't quite right either, as the Euro-Western concept of time does not reflect an Ojibwe conceptualization of time. The Western standard is linear and focused on discrete events, with a primary focus on the future as most important. From an Ojibwe perspective, the past, present, and future are all one and are occurring simultaneously. "All of time is really bunched into the right now," Isaac says. I sit and think on this while we sit by the orange glow of the fire.

Isaac's teachings ask us to return to this moment, in heart, body, mind, and spirit. One way to begin is to simply notice what is present inside and out.

> Inside of me: the pressure behind my eyes.
> Outside of me: the hum of the dryer.
> Inside of me: a memory I didn't expect.
> Outside of me: the smell of wet dog and light bouncing around the window frame.

This movement between inner and outer experience is like gymnastics for the part of us that is capable of observing even the parts that we think are us. The more we move, the more flexible we get. What am I noticing in this moment, both inside of me and around me? Perhaps I can look at them without needing to call any of it good or bad.

As someone who has been through unimaginable hardship, Isaac admits that the here and now and the places we find ourselves in can be pretty awful sometimes, especially when we don't understand the thoughts and emotions that we are having in response to the harsh experiences the world can throw our way. "This is likely why many of us choose to spend so little time maapii," Isaac says while putting his hands on his chest. Pushing our emotions away has consequences, Isaac says. We just keep banking it, and we carry that big bag of burden around on our backs. But every time we acknowledge and sit with those difficult experiences, and breathe them in, the bag gets a little bit easier to carry. "It's like letting a bird out of the cage," he says. "The bird isn't gone, but now it has some room to move around." Isaac leans forward, and I can already tell he is going into story mode . . .

There once was a fisherman who went up and down the shores of the Great Lakes, and even though he worked alone and had just a small boat, he did all right for himself and his family. One morning he goes out a bit farther than usual, hoping to get lucky with his nets in a new spot. While he is preparing his gear, a thick fog rolls in, but not just a regular fog, an absolute wall of white cloud all around his boat through which he can barely see his own hand. His heart begins to race. Being disoriented on the Great Lakes can be a very dangerous thing. He starts to panic, grabbing for the oars and swatting at the fog as if he could clear it away with a big gust.

Then he stops, pulls the oars in, throws out the anchor, and lies down in the boat. While initially he felt like he had been hit by a hurricane, he soon finds the water is calm and there is almost no wind at all. He looks up at the fog and suddenly has an intense feeling of gratitude at how beautiful it is. He breathes the fog in and realizes that it is part of him, it is his breath, the breath of his ancestors, and the breath of all things on the earth. And he nearly missed it all in his frantic effort to get away from it.

Isaac's story about the fisherman lost in the fog has stayed with me. There's something in it that speaks to the way many of us deal with pain: paddling harder, trying to beat back the confusion, swatting at the air as though contentment and clarity can be forced into place. That image of the fisherman setting down the oars, breathing deeply, and allowing the fog to surround him carries a teaching that reaches beyond the story itself. It holds the possibility of resting within uncertainty. It shows us that stillness can reveal what struggle conceals.

As you reflect on your own journey, you might begin to notice what the fog looks like in your life. What does it feel like when your fog closes in? And what kind of person do you want to be in that moment? Do you reach for the oars, tighten your grip, and swing away? Or is there a moment when you pause, even briefly, and allow yourself to just breathe it in?

Isaac talks a lot about breath. I often replay his reminders in my mind. Sometimes it's a simple cue to slow down. Often, his advice comes with a soundtrack. "You can always put on a good ole-fashioned powwow Indian song!" (Check out Isaac's song titled "Indian Song"; it's pretty deadly.) Our traditional songs, burning our medicines, all *great* ways of bringing the body and attention back into the present. As he once put it, "Stop and breathe in what Shkaakaamikwe, Mother Earth, offers us."

Isaac also shares that Elders speak of breath as sacred from the very beginning of life. In Ojibwe teachings, he explains, we come into this world from the stars, and our first breath marks our arrival. Through Ceremony and daily practice, he says, we return to that moment again and again. For those of us who struggle to stay grounded in the present, breath can be a gentle and reliable place to begin.

Isaac often described breath as inseparable from the heart. To illustrate this, he speaks about Anishinaabe pictography, where lines are drawn between beings to show connection. In many of these images, a line runs from the heart of one figure, out through the mouth, and into the heart of another. These lines do not represent speech alone, but relationship. They show how meaning, intention, and presence move between us.

If we were to capture this moment in pictograph, there would be a drawing of me sitting and typing these words out, a line going from my heart, out of my mouth, and into this old Hermes typewriter. Then there would be a picture of you reading this book, the line jumping off of the page, into your mouth, and down into your heart.

As Isaac once said, "Our breath takes the stuff in our heart where it needs to go." I've come to understand this as a form of communication that reaches beyond words alone. In the teachings of many nations, and increasingly in contemporary science, the heart is understood as doing far more than pumping blood. Researchers are saying that the heart is the new brain, that it responds to things before our thoughts have registered what is happening. I think that makes good sense.

When I visualize this teaching, I imagine breath as a line moving outward from the heart, carrying what we hold within us into relationship. It travels through our bodies, into our words, and outward into the world. And of course, connection does not start and stop with other people. It extends to animals, to the land, and to the larger living systems we are part of.

These ways of understanding relationship have often been diminished within Western education, which tends to privilege separation and analysis over connection. Indigenous education, by contrast, teaches us to see ourselves as participants in a living ecosystem. The lines in pictography remind us that our connections are both spiritual and physical, linking us to one another and to all living things.

Follow the path of your breath. If you're up for a little more weirdness, find a space where you can sit comfortably without interruption, even if for just a few minutes. When you are ready, take a few slow, deep breaths. Feel the cool air entering through your nostrils, filling your lungs, and the warm air exiting as you exhale. Continue breathing in and out, allowing your breath to take on its natural pace without any need to change it. Now, imagine a long piece of cloth wrapping softly around your heart in a gentle embrace. Imagine the cloth has been woven together with flexible, glowing strands of energy. It can be any colour you like. It is warm, calming, and comforting.

Take a deep and slow breath. Each time you breathe in, this energy enters your body, moves smoothly in through your nose, into your lungs, around your heart, and then down into your belly. When you breathe out, notice as this warming energy rises upwards, back into your chest, up into your head, soothing any tension or aches that might be there behind your eyes. Notice as the energy makes its way out of your mouth and nose, and out into the world in front of you, following the path of your breath. With each breath, the energy travels further forward with a soft glow and a very gentle movement back and forth.

Take another breath in, and again notice how the energy embraces your heart, lungs, stomach, and other organs, radiating its healing energy through your back and muscles as it goes. Notice how your belly rises as it travels through you. With each breath in and out, imagine the energy's journey extending further and further forward, moving out into the environment around you, exploring each surface and corner, wrapping itself around each item like a curious animal.

Keep breathing. The energy carries a message from your heart, like a telephone line. Watch as this long piece of cloth-like energy makes its way outside, connecting with the grass and trees, and pulsing their energies back towards you, back into your nose, up and around your head, and down into your heart, lungs, and stomach. With each exhale, send out your inner warmth, kindness, and compassion along the line of cloth, into those trees, down into their roots, and high up into their branches and leaves.

Notice how the cloth seems to split into many threads, reaching out like a beautiful creeping vine touching the earth, bringing it your heart message, and sending the heart messages of those living beings back to you. Touch the birds that fly by and feel the energy that you share with them. Watch as your length of energy finds the water and touches stone and plant and rushes along with the waves and currents. Keep breathing, gradually extending the cloth from your heart out into the world, touching all living beings.

Now watch as it connects to the hearts of the people close to you, your family and community, those you love and care for, and those you don't yet know. Breathe out and feel the intentions of your heart, the kindness and gratitude pulsing out to those beings. Breathe in and notice the sensation of their warm energy making its way back to you, all through your mind, body, heart, and spirit. Continue to breathe slowly, while noticing both your interconnectedness with all life and your presence in your body, here and now. Look around the room, feel your feet flat on the floor, and bring movement back into your hands and feet.

If you wish, take a moment to journal about your experience. Write about the sensations, emotions, and insights that arose during this activity. Where did your length of cloth travel? What did it send out and receive? How can your breath and heart influence your sense of presence in daily life?

If you speak to Isaac for even a few minutes, you can bet money he will inevitably speak about relationship. Isaac explains that while a Western scientific perspective often identifies a subject and then works to break it down into its smallest possible parts, an Anishinaabe worldview moves in the opposite direction. According to Isaac, an Anishinaabe system of inquiry "starts with a subject and ends up in the stars." This is why, when speaking with Elders and people who think and speak in Indigenous languages, conversations often branch outward before circling back to the original topic. For those unfamiliar with the culture, this can be difficult to follow, as greater emphasis is placed on how things are related than on their component parts, sequences, or causal chains.

This way of thinking also applies to people. Isaac often says that we are threaded into the ecological fabric of existence, that our thoughts, feelings, bodies, and spirits are always in contact with the world around us. When we experience ourselves as part of something larger, a sense of belonging can emerge. The land, the waters, and the more-than-human world are no longer separate from us, but active participants in our lives.

Isaac once described this by pointing to water. Rivers, he explained, sustain everything they touch, moving continuously without effort or agenda. When we remember that our own bodies are largely made of the same water, it becomes easier to feel those connections as something lived rather than abstract. From this perspective, relationship is not something we create after the fact. It is something we are already inside of.

Isaac stresses the importance of having a sense of belonging. He is confident that when people come to understand who they are and what they are connected to, their quality of life improves and life feels more fulfilling. When I ask how this kind of reconnection can begin, Isaac suggests starting by turning towards ourselves.

He encourages people to notice the good parts of who they are, to gather those pieces together, and to seek out others who carry good relationships and good values. He emphasizes the importance of community, any community, so long as it is rooted in care and meaning. Connection with other people matters deeply. We are meant to be part of something larger than ourselves. Isaac also speaks about the importance of understanding one's spirit. He believes that many people hold on to painful stories about themselves, stories shaped by trauma, loss, or shame. Narratives like "I'm a failure," "I'm broken," or "I'm not good enough" can completely take over how we see ourselves. He shares that spirit names, clans, and helpers offer a very different way of understanding who we are. Rather than anchoring identity in what has hurt us, these teachings point us towards strengths, gifts, and responsibilities.

To explain this, Isaac sometimes talks about animal helpers. If someone carries the spirit of the bear, for example, the qualities associated with the bear become part of how that person understands themselves. Protection, wisdom, and knowledge of medicines begin to shape how they move through the world. From this perspective, identity opens up beyond trauma-based labels and becomes grounded in relationship and purpose. Isaac explains that knowing one's helper helps bring things into perspective and keeps a person rooted in the present.

I'm drawn to the idea of seeking our spirit names, clans, gifts, helpers, and colours as a starting point, in part because this is what set me on my own journey of reconnection. Knowing ourselves in this way has a grounding effect. It gives us something steady to hold on to as we face what is in front of us now. Unlike the restrictive "I am" stories we often repeat to ourselves, these teachings are expansive and layered, carrying more meaning than one could hope to learn in a lifetime.

What's in a name? As I mentioned when we first met, my name is Northern Lights Horse. My helpers are the Loon, Eagle, Horse, and Chickadee. My colours are white and all the colours of the northern lights. I am so much more than the limiting stories my mind has created about me.

Isaac clarifies that "belonging doesn't mean you have to have a super-sacred name, be in a special club, a tribe, a clan, or a famous family to be someone. There is a lot of good medicine in those things, but many of our relatives don't have any of those." He's absolutely right. The colonial system was designed to separate us from our families and our culture, and in many instances, it was (and still is) effective in doing this. But belonging means more than the names and titles; it means belonging to the earth, to the people you interact with each day, to all the people you have known in your past or will know in the future, to the people waiting in the soup line in another town.

"It'd be great to have a big family and have everyone over for a nice barbecue every Sunday and bring the macaroni salad," Isaac says with tongue in cheek, "but this isn't the reality for very many of our relatives, so this shouldn't be the benchmark of connection. Connection is about how often we are in relationship with all of the things around us; the language teaches us this." I like the way Isaac talks, and I can see why so many people listen to his teachings.

Isaac often highlights the important role of Indigenous language in our personal and collective healing. In the Algonquin language family, rather than things being masculine and feminine as you might find in the Romance language family, things are identified as animate and inanimate, and not the things that might generally be considered animate or inanimate from a Euro-Western perspective.

"Our language tells us that our house has a spirit," Isaac shares. "A school is alive and has a spirit, the rocks, trees, and waters are alive and have spirit, and we are in relationship with all of them." This perspective reflects a deeper spiritual and philosophical understanding of the universe, where all things have spirit and are part of a broader network of relationship.

Importantly, Isaac reminds us that this interconnectivity doesn't discriminate on the nature of our experiences or the things it is connected to. Our difficult experiences are all connected to one another as well, and like a string of lights, when one is switched on, the glow spreads to all the other memories, words, and feelings that have occurred before it. So to be interconnected is also to be willing to be connected to things that can be challenging.

Isaac reminds us that this stuff takes practice and is very difficult to do on our own. This is where our relatives and helpers, Elders, Healers, and Ceremony come in. We heal only as a collective, and never alone. Isaac also makes it clear that the present moment isn't an excuse to shirk our accountability to our relatives and to Creation (i.e., it doesn't matter if it's in the past). We have to be conscientious to have good relationships, and we need good relationships to live a good life. So "if you've done someone wrong, make it right," Isaac says. "Give a gift, apologize, make it right."

While Isaac is a deep thinker, he is not one to spend his days in abstraction. He is a man of action, a fierce activist, and a proponent of the Land Back movement. For Isaac, Land Back is people returning and finding their place within living systems of land, law, and responsibility, and the restoration of Indigenous authority in places where it was taken through force, policy, and extraction. He reminds us that the disconnection facing Indigenous Peoples across the world is not accidental or psychological in origin. Colonialism produced this disconnection through land theft, broken treaties, coerced dependency, and the displacement of Indigenous governance. These conditions fractured identity and purpose and continue to cause great harm in our communities. Even as we learn to turn inward with willingness and presence, Isaac insists we stay attentive to the very real external conditions that sustain suffering. Much harm is structural and ongoing and requires action in the real world to remedy.

* * *

As I start the drive away from Nimkii Aazhibikoong, the sky is bright pink and my mind is still back there sitting by the fire with Isaac. It'll be years before I am able to process and appreciate the depth of everything he said, but a few things are already resonating with me. Isaac has a welcoming spirit. He works hard to empower others, to provide support where he can, and to create inclusive environments where more people can get involved and benefit. He encourages collaboration and solution-focused thinking, even when the issues are complex or contentious. For example, Isaac is open to teachings from Elders and Knowledge Keepers from all walks of life. If your message is one of love, connection, and respect for Creation, there is room for you in Isaac's world. This isn't inconsequential.

When it comes to identity, there is a significant amount of tension within community and family and inside of many individuals. This is one of the primary manifestations of colonization and intergenerational trauma that I see in my clinical practice: Indigenous people struggling with their place in both the Western and the Indigenous worlds.

Many of us struggle with feeling like we don't fit within primarily white spaces, whether those be schools, workplaces, or social circles. There is definitely overt racism that threatens our safety in these spaces, but there are also the more subtle forms of psychological segregation that occur, the microaggressions and undercurrent of exclusion and discomfort that exist just below the surface. Sometimes it is present in the contrast we feel when hearing about the challenges that our non-Indigenous friends and colleagues are experiencing. Not that they are less, but that they are different.

As an Indigenous person, when you hear about weekend plans, family disputes, or things that your colleagues are struggling with, it doesn't take long to realize that you are coming from a very different world. All families have conflict, addiction, and estrangement. All families have secrets, and all families have pain and loss. But not all families have missing and murdered mothers, daughters, aunties, and sisters. Not all families have such a high frequency of death by suicide, overdose, or violence. Not all families have members who are living in abject poverty without heating in the winter, with no access to clean drinking water, and with high exposure to environmental neurotoxins. Not all families have had their languages forcefully eradicated or their cultural practices made illegal and punished with physical abuse and imprisonment. Not all families have had the bones of their ancestors dug up and put on display in museums for others to enjoy. It shouldn't come as a surprise that at our core, many Indigenous people feel disconnected from the social majority.

I think about the image of Isaac showing up to a family barbecue wearing a golf shirt and khaki shorts holding a macaroni salad, and chuckle to myself. With this simple picture and his signature laugh, Isaac has touched on something critical: that our identity as Indigenous peoples cannot be measured on a Western standard. Our definition of family cannot be based on the nuclear family structure. Our meaning of connection cannot be reduced to names, labels, and organizational involvement. It is altogether different. The metrics are different. The foundations are different.

Indigenous identity also cannot be measured solely on our past. Western society has a habit of painting Indigenous peoples as a culture frozen in time. The collective consciousness sees Indigeneity as something that existed once long ago but not anymore. The stoic young brave looking out over the land with bow and arrow in hand (the "I just killed a buffalo" face). But this isn't an accurate representation of what it is to be Indigenous in North America either. Culture is dynamic, never staying still long enough to allow someone to study it or sketch a representative portrait. And for Indigenous peoples, the experience of five hundred years of genocide, forced assimilation, and structural racism has complicated things considerably.

How native is really native? To be a "real Indian," do you have to be born on a reservation? Do you have to have grown up there? Do you have to live there now? Do you have to have dark-brown skin, high cheekbones, and long jet-black hair? Do you have to know how to hunt? Do you have to attend Ceremony regularly? Do you have to know your language? Do you have to be a member of a federally recognized tribe or band? Do you have to carry your Indian Status card in your wallet?

Sidebar: Once, while showing her Indian Status card to a particularly crusty clerk at a cash register, my mom was informed that her status card had expired, to which my mom sarcastically celebrated at a volume that mortified teenage me, "Well, I guess I'm a white woman now!" Hilarious now, but at the time, I wanted to crawl into a hole and die. I feel pride when I think about it now. Funny how things change.

In *Disciplined Hearts*, Theresa O'Nell introduces the concept of the *empty centre* to conceptualize the evaluation of identity struggles within Indigenous communities. At the centre of the circle is the core of community identity, the "true" Indigenous identity. This core is represented by the past, by tradition, by an image of authentic Indigenous identity, unscathed by external influence. As one gets farther and farther from the circle, they are less and less legitimately Indigenous. To be outside of the circle is to be non-Indigenous. But the centre is an illusion, it is empty. The image that has been constructed there doesn't actually exist and is unattainable. Genocide, colonization, assimilation, cultural change, and time have made it impossible to be in the centre. But this doesn't mean that we don't fight to get as close to or as far away from that vacant centre as possible. Our relatives struggle equally with trying to change themselves to belong within white spaces as they do trying to belong within Indigenous spaces.

Sitting in a university classroom with some Indigenous and non-Indigenous students, all who have grown up in the city, I might imagine myself to be pretty close to the centre of that empty circle. I have a status card. I was born in the Far North. Nīhithawīwin is my mother's first language. I checked the rabbit snares with nōhkom as a boy. Pretty soon I'm starting to feel like the painting of that stoic warrior looking out across the plains. But fast forward a couple of weeks to when I'm up at the Sun Dance with my relatives, and holy smokes, do I feel like a pale city slicker! Now I find myself far from the empty centre.

It's important to touch on something that growing up, I never would have expected to be such a pervasive problem. While many are doing the hard and honest work of reconnecting, healing, and learning to carry our responsibilities, there are some who falsely claim an Indigenous identity without any real connection to the communities they name. These actions cause harm. They take up space that is meant for Indigenous people, reshape stories that aren't theirs to tell, and create confusion in places where clarity and trust are already fragile. It isn't always easy to name, especially when those actions come wrapped in good intentions and echo the language of people who are genuinely trying to find their way back to family and culture after generations of forced separation; but it matters. Our cultural identities are not personal preferences or expressions. They are rooted in kinship, territory, story, and accountability to community. In this sense, false claims to Indigenous identity are not harmless misunderstandings; they are a particularly insidious form of colonial violence.

These tensions reflect just how complex Indigenous identity has become. In O'Nell's conceptualization, our identity is constantly in flux. It is a product of its context and is determined by relationship. I think this perspective fits well with the teachings about presence, especially when it comes to an Indigenous conceptualization of the self. From a nēhīthāwāk perspective, the self is relational, inseparable from community and Creation, and consisting of a spiritual essence that persists beyond physical life.

Isaac offers two very important teachings here. First, the whole idea of "self" as it is used in Western psychological dialogue may be at odds with an Indigenous view of personhood. We are more than this one set of mind, body, and spirit. Our boundaries are permeable and connect us to others in a single "ecological fabric of existence." The differences our minds perceive between us and the rest of Creation is an illusion. The more we are able to see ourselves as connected to and part of, rather than as a singular self defined by the labels we collect, the more aware we can become of how they might be limiting our options. Second, Isaac points to our teachings and traditions as a rich source of that connectivity. I have tens of thousands of Bear Clan family members from hundreds of nations all across Turtle Island. My helpers connect me to Mother Nature, and my name reaches across generations. These are things that we can find with help from others. Things that even those who find themselves very far from that vacant centre can touch and feel once again part of, rather than separate from.

When I reflect on my own journey of belonging, I have certainly struggled. I recall attending ceremonies, social events, and protests as a child. My mom likes to tell a story about how at four years old, I insisted upon joining the men in a Pipe Ceremony during a protest at the legislative buildings in Winnipeg, Manitoba. I have a vague memory of sitting in the circle and the burst of laughter of the men when it was my turn with the Pipe. I guess I was trying hard to look extra sacred, as if it were something I had done a thousand times, which they found very amusing. I remember being so proud of being Cree as a kid. I showed off the beaded jacket my mother and grandmother had sewn for me, and even tried to demonstrate some of my nonexistent powwow dancing skills at a talent show audition in third grade, which, thank Creator, I was not selected for! Those judges saved me from a lifetime of teasing.

But things changed as I got older. I found myself avoiding these events in my teenage years and speaking less openly about my Indigeneity at school or with friends. We had moved farther west into the prairies, and I experienced a lot more racism in those years. Overt and unabashed racist comments from students, teachers, and strangers were now the norm, as was being followed around and searched in stores or stopped by the police and told to turn out my pockets. I've been stopped and told to empty my pockets about twenty times in my life. I never realized how messed up that is until I found out that this doesn't happen to most people, that most people have never been stopped by police while walking down the street or standing with their friends. People would yell slurs from their car windows and even throw things at my brother and me on our walk home from school. I was about ten years old when we moved. When I imagine this happening to my son, who is ten now, it makes me feel ill, but that's how it was. And in many places where there are lots of Indigenous people, that's how it still is.

So perhaps as the result of some internalized oppression, some mix of fear and shame, survival instinct, or a desire to fit in, I found myself drifting away from my Indigenous identity. I had begun to associate my Indigeneity with my experience of racism and the many crises and losses our family experienced.

News of suicide, homicide, overdose, violence, drowning, or an accident involving a relative are much too common in our families and communities. I think many Indigenous people feel a twinge of anxiety when receiving a phone call from a relative that they haven't heard from in a while, and that is a truly horrible thing. Before calling me, my brother typically texts first with "Got time for a call?" and then adds the qualifier "Nobody died, everything is fine." For these reasons, which I now recognize as a manifestation of intergenerational trauma, I separated myself from my cultural identity for many years.

There were exceptions, of course. Each year my parents would cram the eight of us kids into the back of a rusty Suburban and drive fifteen hours north of Winnipeg to the territory of our ancestors, to a small blue cabin, to fishing camps, and to days spent out on an island or in the bush. While on the land with my aunties, uncles, and cousins, all those insecurities would slip away and I would feel whole again, for at least a while. But I even began avoiding those trips as a teenager, and before too long I felt very far from my culture and community. I have a lot of regret for the lost time I should have spent in the North.

Years later, now an adult and a father, I found a renewed motivation to reconnect to the land and to my relatives. I wanted my children to feel what I had felt in those early years. I wanted them to look out on the lake and feel their heart flutter like mine had. I wanted to see them put their tobacco down to greet the lake, give gratitude, and to wrap up their spirits by saying goodbye to the lake when it was time to leave. I wanted them to be proud of being nisichawayasi nehethowuk. So I made a point to find what I had left behind.

I recall attending my first Sweat Lodge Ceremony around the time my daughter was born, and hearing the sound of the drum in my ears and the pounding of my heart like the voice of an old friend. In the years that followed, I built relationships with as many Knowledge Keepers as I could, to listen and learn, to bring my new family out to the lands of my ancestors, and to be in Ceremony. I fasted out on the land several times a year, attended sweats wherever I could find them, and listened intently to the teachings of Elders and Knowledge Keepers.

While writing this I realize I make this reconnection sound both quick and easy, though it was anything but. I experienced enormous anxiety throughout this entire process and found myself panicking while attending Ceremony on a number of occasions. In reality, this was a slow reintroduction that took the better part of a decade and was full of apprehension, imposter syndrome, and self-doubt.

My mother had been asking me to attend the Sun Dance Ceremony for years, not pressuring me, just indicating that there was a spot for me if I so chose. For a long time, I chose not to. The idea of looking my suppressed pain directly in the face in the presence of a bunch of other traumatized Indians for four days in the hot sun horrified me. I felt like I didn't belong in those spaces, that I had been away too long to come back. But eventually, after attending the final day of the Ceremony at a family medicine camp one summer, I offered my tobacco and made my commitment to dance. I am not a Knowledge Keeper, and it is not my place to speak of the specifics of the Sun Dance Ceremony here, but I believe it has had a significant impact on my life.

So if you're wrestling with identity, know that you're not alone in this struggle. Maybe you've felt the sting of not being "rez enough" in some spaces, or being "too rez" in others. Perhaps you've caught yourself trying to measure up to some impossible standard of authenticity, only to realize that the target keeps moving. It's a common and familiar experience, this code-switching dance between worlds, and it can leave you feeling exhausted, disconnected, and unsure about who you are. But identity is ultimately about your ancestors and the community that claims you now.

The beauty of our Indigenous identity is that it's resilient and adaptive. We have survived centuries of attempts to erase us, and we continue to thrive in new and unexpected ways. So consider embracing the complexity of your identity. Allow yourself to be a bridge between worlds, carrying the wisdom of your ancestors while navigating the realities of contemporary life. Your journey of self-discovery and cultural reconnection is valid, no matter where you are on that path.

6.

VIVIAN RECOLLET

Now we head to Tkaronto, where we find Grandmother Vivian Recollet holding a sharing circle at a local community centre. Vivian is a Turtle Clan Elder from Wiikwemkoong Unceded Territory. She is Anishinaabe and has worked as a nurse and helper for many years, dedicating her life to walking with people experiencing homelessness and struggling with substance use in the downtown core.

Many don't realize this, but Toronto has a massive Indigenous population, with as many as sixty thousand people identifying as First Nations, Inuit, or Métis. Vivian is a Sixties Scoop survivor and an Indian Day School survivor. The Sixties Scoop refers to a period of about twenty years beginning in the early 1960s when the Canadian government began the very gradual (forty-year) closure of residential schools and simultaneously accelerated a policy of mass apprehension and adopting out of Indigenous children to non-Indigenous families. Similar policies were also being enacted within the United States.

Children were sent as far as countries in Europe, with adopting families sometimes paying for the child after selecting them in catalogue-like brochures. While many children were adopted out to loving and well-intentioned families, many others were not so lucky. Some survivors of the Sixties Scoop have described horrific experiences of abuse and discrimination at the hands of their adopted families. In some cases, children were adopted for the purpose of slave labour on farms. These apprehensions and subsequent adoptions occurred without the consent of the biological families, often under coercive circumstances, with the vast majority of children being sent to non-Indigenous homes far from their communities. In addition to the physical, emotional, and sexual abuse that many children experienced, the Sixties Scoop also had the devastating effect of alienating the children from their cultures. Survivors grew up not belonging in the world they were raised in, but also not belonging in the world from which they were stolen.

Sadly, this practice did not end with the Sixties Scoop. It continues today through what many refer to as the Millennium Scoop, where children are apprehended en masse by the child welfare system and placed in foster care. In fact, there are more First Nations children separated from their families by the child welfare system than there ever were within residential schools. The physical and cultural genocide Indigenous Peoples have experienced at the hands of Canada's partnership of church and state are often on Vivian's mind as she does her work. Vivian describes the extreme harm of colonization as the source of suffering for Indigenous Peoples. She believes that the residential school system, the Sixties Scoop, today's child welfare system, and the systemic racism present in virtually all areas of modern life have been incredibly debilitating, creating a revolving door of trauma, homelessness, and addiction.

Another tragic consequence of these systems, Vivian shares, is a widespread pattern of emotional suppression in our communities, which is being passed on from generation to generation. The children who attended residential schools were severely punished for crying, for laughing, for screaming when afraid, or for demonstrating affection to one another (even simple physical touch like hand-holding between siblings was prohibited and punished with physical and psychological abuse). Vivian shares that many of our relatives learned quickly, as a matter of survival, to suppress all emotion, to not feel, to not share, to not love. Those survivors brought those suppression skills home and, as parents, unintentionally handed them down to their children and grandchildren.

Vivian walks with people who have endured immense adversity. Physical, emotional, and sexual abuse histories are almost a guarantee in this population. Many have repeatedly witnessed the deaths of their friends and family by overdose, suicide, and homicide. Most are far from home and using substances to find a moment of relief from intense physical and psychological pain.

From Vivian's perspective, experiential avoidance is first and foremost about protecting ourselves. When we don't understand painful thoughts, emotions, or sensations, sometimes the safest thing to do is to escape by ignoring, distracting, or dulling the experience in some way. But our methods of protecting ourselves from these experiences can be destructive for us and those around us.

Vivian says that many of us wear our pain and trauma like a big protective blanket over our shoulders. "Everywhere we go, everything we do, every person we talk to, the blanket is there as the focal point. We are constantly aware of the blanket, we tell everyone how hot and itchy the blanket is until they don't want to hear about it anymore, and we let it get in the way of the things we want to accomplish. It's hard to plant a garden, go for a swim, or cook dinner for a friend with this big, bulky blanket in the way." But it doesn't make sense to throw the blanket out either; it does get cold from time to time, after all, and we've grown quite fond of it. Perhaps we can fold the blanket and put it down while we plant those tomatoes or do a cannonball into the lake. It isn't gone, but it doesn't stop us from living our lives.

One purpose that pain serves, according to Vivian, is giving us the ability to help someone else down the road. Being able to speak to an experience and to let others know that they are not alone can be powerful. Vivian talks about the circles she holds where participants are welcome to share their struggles openly, to cry, and to relate to one another. Vivian says it would be strange for her to sit in a circle or work with people whose primary struggle is hoarding, as she hasn't had that experience and would not be able to understand that kind of pain, but that she could easily walk with someone who is struggling with alcohol use, domestic abuse, or the loss of a child, as these are things that have impacted her life and are forms of pain that can sit with the pain of the other person.

Vivian spends a lot of time in circle. The circle is an opportunity to share our experiences and to take part in collective healing. There are things that we ourselves might not be ready to acknowledge or to sit with, but we may be able to hear and acknowledge those things in another. Sitting with the pain of another can be healing and teach us how to be with those emotions until we are ready to share.

I remember asking Vivian about her thoughts on mindfulness and similar concepts. What are the benefits of accessing the present moment and finding a version of ourselves that transcends the many labels our mind has for us? Vivian shares a story of being invited to sing traditional songs for a charity event that was being held at a local church. She recalls being sat in the second-row pew, directly behind a group of nuns, and having a sudden intense urge to escape.

She turned to the drummers and said, "We gotta get out of here," and felt a sudden bolt of fear shoot up her arms, into her neck, and then to the back of her head. Next, she recalls feeling a blow to the head, with actual pain as though she had been physically struck. She now knows that this was a flashback of being beaten by a nun at the Indian Day School she attended. She asked her son who was there to stand in front of her so she could look into his eyes and be grounded in the present, as a reminder that she was a mother and a grandmother, not a little girl being abused.

This event is important to her, the cause is important, and having the traditional songs heard is important. She sings loudly while holding the painful memory and keeping herself from time-travelling by locking on her adult son and the sound of the drum. Vivian says that when someone is going through intense pain and suffering, all we can do is support them in getting through that moment and remind them that they are here, with us, in the present, that they are safe. It is critical when we face pain, old or new, that we do it here in the present, because our mind can lead us to all sorts of places.

If you are carrying something heavy right now, it may help to pause and gently ask, What am I noticing in this moment? How is my mind labelling this experience? See if you can look at it without needing to label any of it good or bad. From this place of presence, you might also ask, What roles or labels am I clinging to right now? How are they influencing my actions or decisions? There's no need to push the answers away. Just listening for a response is a powerful start.

* * *

People who have lived through traumatic experiences often find themselves back there in their minds, caught in a steady stream of "if only," "why me," and "I am" thoughts. These are usually paired with painful emotions, vivid images, and physical sensations. Our minds are skilled at handing us labels: I am depressed. I am a mess. I am too much. I am not enough. I am bad. I am empty. I am nothing. These stories can become so familiar that they follow us through our day, often without us noticing.

What "I am" stories has your mind spoken to you today, even in the background? The next time you notice one, you could pause and ask, Is this true in every moment, with every person, in every place, no matter what? Most of the time, the answer will be no. Even this small moment of noticing can create a little space between us and the "I am" stories we have been tangled up in.

When the mind starts to bring up its old stories, it can help to sit and ask: What roles or stories about myself am I trying to protect right now? Why does this one feel so urgent? Sometimes simply noticing that we are defending a certain version of ourselves reveals what is tender underneath. The strongest stories are often wrapped around the softest places. And sometimes the story is less about identity and more about protection, guarding something inside that has not had space to be safely seen in a long time.

As with difficult emotional experiences, it can help to give these stories a name, something playful or gentle. "There goes my old friend self-doubt with the 'I am a failure' story. He's always early for these meetings." These small naming moments can shift the way we relate to our stories, turning them from fixed truths into passing visitors. We do not have to fight them or prove them wrong. We can let them be here and still choose how we want to move forward.

Who am I? Like Isaac, Vivian shared that presence also requires an understanding of who you are and where you come from. What nation do you belong to? What territory does that nation call home?

What is your spirit name? What is your clan, and what responsibilities does that clan carry within the community? But given the harms of colonization, Vivian acknowledged that it can be difficult to stay present in this way. When people are focused on survival, as many of our relatives are, that deeper knowledge of place, identity, and responsibility can be pushed aside.

As she explained it, grounding ourselves becomes much harder when our footing feels uncertain. Still, Vivian is far from pessimistic. She believes deeply in our capacity to heal, and in the presence of healing opportunities all around us. She often spoke about the power of reconnection and of returning to the beauty of our cultures. Witnessing people find their voices again, she said, is one of the most meaningful parts of the work. There is something powerful in seeing individuals speak their experiences aloud and share how they arrived where they are now, and to say it among others without shame.

In those moments where our mind tells us we are alone, it may be helpful to ask ourselves, Who or what around me is offering support in this moment, whether I can feel it or not? Sometimes the drum, the wind, or even the memory of a kind word can remind us that we're not walking alone.

To Vivian, reconnection to Creation is a fundamental part of honouring and respecting our spirits. Offering tobacco, walking by the water, and singing our song to the water are simple but meaningful practices. She speaks of these acts as gifts, reminders that relationship is always available to us. As I remember it, Vivian once said that sometimes we need to reconnect with our first mother, Mother Earth, before we can reconnect with our human family. In her teachings, land and water are not separate from our emotional lives, but deeply woven into them.

Vivian compares our attempts to regulate and control our emotions to trying to regulate and control the tide. Each time you go and sit by the water, it will be different. Some days the surface is calm. Other days it flows quickly or unpredictably. She encourages paying attention to what the mind is saying and how the heart feels, without trying to force those currents to flow in any particular direction. The water teaches us about the pace of healing, and that rather than seeking control, we should seek presence.

Vivian highlights the interconnectedness of all beings and stresses the importance of recognizing and respecting our relationship with Mother Earth and the animals, plants, waters, and seasons. She explains that by acknowledging the gifts of Creation and practising reciprocity, we can build deeper relationships with one another as human beings, and with ourselves.

As I remember it, she put it this way: "We are small. Just tiny beings in this great big universe. Our role might seem small or insignificant, but we are connected to everything else. When we truly recognize Creation and the many gifts we receive, it becomes clear that we are not separate. We are part of that larger circle of life."

Vivian discusses the difference in perspective between Western conceptualizations of the mind, emotions, body, and spirit, and an Anishinaabe understanding of the self. She emphasizes that within an Anishinaabe worldview, these are not separate categories, but parts of a whole that are always in relationship. As she explained to me, "We don't compartmentalize ourselves." We are not divided into physical, emotional, mental, and spiritual selves, but understood as connected to Creation. Vivian shared how this understanding became real for her during her first fasting ceremony.

Alone on the land, she began to feel herself in direct relationship with what surrounded her. She became aware of the ground beneath her, the cool air on her skin, the living and crawling world around her, and the warmth of the sun. In that experience, she came to recognize herself as part of something much larger than she had previously understood. Through that moment, Vivian began to see herself as connected not only to the plants and the land, but also to the sky world and the stars that hold such an important place in Anishinaabe teachings. These stories speak to where we come from and how we belong.

Vivian often reflects on how rarely we are given the space to remember this kind of connection and how easily it can slip from view in the pace of everyday life. I remember her saying something like "in that moment, I understood how small I was, not in a way that made me feel less than, but in a way that showed me I was part of something much bigger. I was connected to the plants, the sky, the stars, the Milky Way. That's how I began to understand myself. We are deeply connected, but we don't often slow down enough to remember that."

Vivian shares that when our mind, body, and spirit are aligned and strong, nothing can break us. She shares a teaching of the Medicine Wheel, where emotional, mental, physical, and spiritual aspects of our being are considered and balanced. The Medicine Wheel serves as a powerful tool for self-reflection, problem-solving, and personal growth. "Those four quadrants—emotional, physical, mental, and spiritual—describe who we are as a united whole. The idea that our thoughts, that mental quadrant, can somehow be separated from those other parts is an illusion, and not a very useful one."

As the conversation draws to a close, Vivian reflects on the importance of this inner alignment. "The distance from the head to the heart is very short, but it's important to work to keep them together. Our minds are a sponge, taking in the media and voices of others and the things that we see, good things, bad things, and it is easy for us to get very overwhelmed by these." This insight encapsulates the essence of Vivian's message, highlighting the ongoing effort required to maintain coherence between our thoughts, feelings, bodies, and spirit and to view the self as a part of something infinite and unbreakable.

* * *

I thank Vivian for sharing her knowledge and story with me so openly and look forward to when we will see each other again. I hop on the streetcar headed east on Queen Street while Vivian's words echo between my ears. Vivian has likely never heard of psychological flexibility, self-as-context, the observer self, or any of the other psychological jargon we love to throw around in psychotherapy, but she has a master's grasp of the concepts and practices.

Vivian described herself as "a spirit on a human journey." This perspective encourages us to recognize a part of ourselves that observes and integrates our thoughts, feelings, bodies, and histories without being defined by them. Vivian's teaching invites us to remember what endures. How has my spirit remained constant through all the changes of my life? What does that constancy tell me about who I really am?

Each of us is on a journey. Vivian's view invites us to see ourselves as more than our momentary experiences or the labels society places on us. It offers a sense of continuity, particularly powerful for those of us grappling with the impacts of colonization and intergenerational trauma. We aren't our histories; we aren't our traumas; we aren't even our minds or bodies. There is a deeper self that sustains all our experiences and is connected to all of Creation, a spiritual self.

Vivian's teachings emphasize the importance of connection to the land and engagement in Ceremony as pathways to grounding and presence. She spoke of the power inherent in offering tobacco, walking by water, or participating in a sweat lodge. These practices, deeply rooted in our traditions, serve to bring our attention fully into the present moment, guiding us away from dwelling on the past or worrying about the future. Just as water adapts to its environment—flowing around, under, or over obstacles while maintaining its essential nature—we too can learn to move through life's difficulties with flexibility and resilience, always returning to our core selves while responding to whatever our context has in store for us.

Reflecting on my conversation with Vivian, I'm reminded of the pervasive impact of colonization and intergenerational trauma on Indigenous life. It's not history—it's a reality that shapes our everyday experiences. Physically, we see it in the disproportionate rates of homelessness and substance use in our communities. It's in the bodies of our relatives, worn down by stress and trauma, carrying the weight of generations. It's in the scars—visible and invisible—left by residential schools and the foster-care system.

Emotionally, it's a dam built by years of forced suppression. In residential schools, when our grandparents and parents learned to choke back tears, to swallow their laughter, to hide their fear, they brought that emotional armour home, and we've inherited it. Many of us struggle to express affection or process our feelings in healthy ways. Now we carry the blanket of unexpressed emotion, always aware of its presence, always fighting against its weight but unwilling to put it down. We're constantly navigating issues of identity and self-worth, never quite sure where we fit. Flashbacks and trauma responses can be triggered by the most unexpected things—like Vivian's experience in the church. Many of us live with one foot stuck in the past, replaying the "if-onlys" and "why-mes" on an endless loop.

Spiritually, it's a wall that separates us from our traditions. Many of us struggle to connect with the ceremonies that sustained our ancestors. We feel adrift, cut off from the land that once nourished our spirits. It's a constant battle to maintain our sense of belonging, to remember who we are in a world that often seems determined to make us forget.

This is what intergenerational trauma looks like in our lives. It's the revolving door of addiction and homelessness that traps so many of our relatives. It's the struggle to form healthy attachments when our family bonds have been systematically attacked for generations. It's the overrepresentation of our children in foster care and our adults in prisons. It's the chronic health issues stemming from years of unresolved trauma and stress. But it's also in the smaller, everyday moments. It's in the panic that rises when we must interact with institutions that have historically harmed us. It's in the difficulty we have staying present, always braced for the next blow. It's in the way we sometimes struggle to connect with our own children, not knowing how to give the love that our parents and grandparents also struggled to express.

Yet, as Vivian reminded me, there's hope woven through all this pain. Our capacity for healing is as vast as the trauma we've endured. Vivian spoke about "rewriting our story," seeing ourselves as more than the sum of our experiences or the many things we've been told about ourselves. We have the capacity to observe our story as it unfolds, to choose how we interpret our experiences, and to actively shape our narrative moving forward. Every time we share our stories, every time we reconnect with our cultures, every time we sing our songs or offer our tobacco, we're reclaiming pieces of ourselves. We're igniting that spark of *survivance* that has kept our peoples alive through centuries of attempted erasure.

The consequences of intergenerational trauma are heavy, but they are not the end of our story. It's a chapter—sometimes a long, painful chapter—but it's not the whole book. As we heal, reconnect, and remember, we write new chapters. We break cycles, build bridges back to our traditions, and create new pathways for the generations to come. When we look back, we may find that those painful chapters were what made the story great.

I once heard Dr. Brenda Restoule, an Ojibwekwe from Dokis First Nation (and a gifted clinical psychologist), say, "Trauma is not the only thing we transmit intergenerationally; we also transmit intergenerational power." I still get goose bumps when I think of those words. They remind me of Vivian's teaching. To see ourselves as spirits on a human journey is to remember that we carry more than our wounds. We carry the prayers and strengths of those who came before us, the knowledge they protected, and the connections they never let go. That deeper self is still here, steady beneath all the change. When we return to it through story, Ceremony, and the land, we find we have always had what we need to keep going. In living this way, we also pass these strengths forward, so our descendants inherit not only the echoes of our pain, but the fullness of our love, our power, and our ways of belonging.

7.

YOU, HERE, NOW

As we journey deeper into the strange intersection of psychological flexibility and Indigenous helping wisdom, we find ourselves at a crossroads of understanding—where the individual meets the collective, where Indigenous knowledge intersects with contemporary psychology. These differing perspectives present both challenges and opportunities.

In the science of psychological flexibility, we encounter ideas like the "observing self," the part of us that notices our thoughts and feelings without becoming entangled in them. This perspective suggests there's a constant, unchanging part of us that witnesses our ever-changing inner world.

At first glance, this focus on the self might seem at odds with Indigenous worldviews that emphasize our interconnectedness with all of Creation. Yet as we've seen in our conversations with Isaac and Vivian, there are really important teachings about the part of us that transcends our immediate experiences. Isaac spoke of how we are all "threaded into the ecological fabric of existence," suggesting a self that is both individual and part of a greater whole. Vivian emphasized how our mind, body, heart, and spirit are intertwined, forming a united whole that, when aligned, cannot be broken. These teachings offer a rich, nuanced understanding of self that I believe complements and expands upon the concept of the observer self.

Mindfulness is sometimes suggested as a strategy to get rid of stress and worry, but true presence isn't escape. Rather, it's a deepening of our engagement with life in all its complexity, and in recognizing ourselves as part of a vast web of relationships—with our families, our communities, our ancestors, the land, and all living beings—there's a sense of expansiveness. From this perspective, cultivating presence becomes a way of honouring our place within the whole.

This teaching emphasizes the importance of ongoing, nonjudgmental contact with psychological and environmental events as they occur. You don't need to meditate in a dark room for hours or empty your mind completely. Instead, we gradually become more and more conscious of and engaged with our experience with the inner and outer worlds, even when that experience is difficult. Noticing the sights, sounds, and sensations around us, as well as the thoughts, emotions, and bodily sensations within us, while also recognizing that there's a part of us—our spiritual self—that remains constant amid these changing experiences.

By cultivating this kind of presence and understanding of self, we develop greater psychological flexibility. We stay grounded in the present moment and in our true nature, which exists beyond the unpleasant thoughts, feelings, or events. This flexibility allows us to respond to whatever life throws at us in ways that align with our deepest values, rather than simply reacting out of habit or fear.

As we explore what it means to embrace ourselves in the here and now, we can navigate the terrain between individual experience and collective wisdom, and draw upon both the science of psychological flexibility and the teachings of our ancestors. We don't have to force these perspectives to align. We can engage with them critically and creatively, always keeping our cultural values at the forefront. Remember, this is your journey. Take what resonates, leave what doesn't, and always trust the wisdom of your own experience and what your ancestors are telling you. There's no one right way to do healing work. It's an ongoing process, a way of engaging with life that honours both our individual path and our shared story.

As we explore the concept of presence, it's important to repeat that Indigenous perspectives on self and time often differ significantly from Western viewpoints. These differences, deeply embedded in our languages and worldviews, can drastically influence how we understand and experience our world. In many Indigenous cultures, the self is not seen as an isolated entity, but as part of a continuum that extends both backward and forward in time. Our ancestors and descendants are not separate from us, but integral parts of who we are.

Similarly, our understanding of the present moment is often more fluid and expansive than the Western notion of a fixed point in time. For many Indigenous peoples, the past, present, and future are not strictly separated, but coexist and inform each other continuously. And as you'll recall from our chat with Isaac, objects that Western thought considers inanimate—like rocks, trees, or houses—are recognized as having spirit and life. This animacy extends the concept of self beyond the boundaries of the human body, fostering a sense of deep interconnection with and responsibility for all of Creation. This worldview can lead to a form of presence that naturally encompasses a broader span of time, experience, and responsibility.

These perspectives offer a rich, nuanced understanding of self that both challenges and complements Western psychological concepts. Perhaps "being present" involves attending to immediate sensations and thoughts, but also feeling our connection to ancestors, descendants, and the spirit of the world around us. Rather than a detached witness, the "observing self" in this context might be understood as a point of connection, a way of experiencing our place in the web of all relations.

Understanding these cultural and linguistic differences is crucial as we consider the utility of psychological flexibility for Indigenous peoples. It reminds us that our journey towards well-being must be grounded in our own cultural contexts and ways of knowing. It also highlights the potential for Indigenous wisdom to enrich and expand our understanding of what it means to be here now and to be connected to ourselves and the world around us.

RESTORYING YOUR STORY

Stories and symbols stay alive in our bones. They are passed down through words, thoughts, and blood. Both Isaac and Vivian speak in story and rich imagery. They wield story and metaphor as tools with the capacity for great transformation. A story can hold what is hard to say, give shape to feelings we struggle to name, and remind us that understanding takes many forms.

We all carry stories about who we are. Some took shape when we were young, around the time we learned certain truths were best kept quiet or that parts of ourselves should be hidden. Others formed later, in moments of loss, humiliation, or disappointment. These stories shape how we look out at the world, what we welcome, what we avoid, and the way we hold our shoulders in a crowded room. The stories might whisper that we are not enough, that we are too much, that we are bound to fail, or that we must carry the weight of other people's pain. Over time, they feel less like stories and more like facts. They influence our choices, our relationships, and our sense of possibility.

I remember speaking with someone who was holding on to a story about always being "the one left behind." They could trace it back to an early move away from friends, then through breakups, then into job losses. Each event seemed to confirm the story. As we talked, another version started to appear. It still included all the same events, but with a different thread tying them together. In this version, they were not only left behind. They were someone who stayed when others could not, who built stability for the people around them, who learned how to adapt and keep going. The facts did not change. The feelings did not change. But the relationship with the story transformed.

We are always creating narratives and deciding which details matter, how to connect them, and what they mean. Most of the time, we do this without even noticing. Yet when we bring the story into view and see it as something we are making, we open the possibility of telling it differently. Our mind will use this as yet another tactic of experiential avoidance if we let it, so we must remember that the goal isn't to erase the painful story or to find a better, kinder version. The goal is to see that there are many ways to tell a story.

Our ancestors have always understood the changing life of a story. A story shared at one moment might mean something else entirely the next time it is told. We can apply that same skill into our own lives. We can honour where we have been while allowing the story to grow and shift as we do. This is one of the powers of presence: the ability to notice the story we are in and to step gently into another telling of it.

FINDING CENTRE IN CULTURE

When I listen to teachers like Isaac and Vivian, I see people who know how to be present. They have lived through more than most people can imagine. They have learned how to remain here, alive and connected, in the presence of pain that does not explain itself. What they teach does not come from books. It comes from what they have seen and heard and felt, from the land and from the relationships that healed them. This is the kind of wisdom that has nourished our nations over millennia. I would take it over a stack of PhDs any day. Our cultural practices offer good and accessible ways to ground ourselves in the present moment, to see ourselves as something more expansive than just a body or a mind, and to help us become aware of our whole selves, inside and out.

There are of course many ceremonies that foster a compassionate awareness of your experiences, but remember, this book is not the place to learn about Ceremony. But don't be afraid to reach out to an Elder or ceremonial practitioner who is trusted in your community and ask them for a teaching. Just be sure you are doing so in a way that is respectful and in line with the protocols and expectations of the Peoples in that particular place. In my experience, the greatest teachers are kind and open with those who want to learn and come to listen with a good heart. While Ceremony and sacred knowledge are best learned through direct relationship and protocol, there are many everyday ways we can nurture presence based on a worldview that prioritizes interconnection, wholism, and a circular perspective of time, space, and place.

One way many of us are taught to begin is by greeting the morning with gratitude. There is a simple, strong medicine in starting the day this way, acknowledging the breath of life and setting our intentions. If you can, when the sun is rising, it is a good practice to step outside, maybe with a glass of water, and set your thanks and intentions for the day. You can give thanks to all parts of our universe that let us be here, to experience this life: the little crawling insects, the four-legged and winged ones, the winds and waters, the plants and trees, Grandfather Sun and Grandmother Moon. Remember what a gift it is to be alive.

Regular prayer and quiet time for reflection also help us build an appreciation for what is, not just when things are tough, but as a part of our daily life. Taking a moment in your day to just be still, to watch and listen from the stillness of your spirit, can be a very grounding thing. However you pray, that is the right way for you.

I remember one time when I was fasting, I started thinking about all the ways I was connected to everything around me. Just "me and the tree," I thought, looking at a big birch. Soon enough, that circle grew in my mind: "Me, that rock, and the tree." Then "Me, that rock, those clouds, and the tree." It kept going, taking in my family, my community, my nation, all the animals, this whole planet, the entire universe. Even now, just saying to myself, "Me, Lisa, the kids, and the tree," can bring a quick comfort and a sense of belonging. You might try it yourself, starting with who and what is closest to you, and just speaking those connections out loud or in your heart.

My auntie Ivy has a beautiful way with painting rocks. She will sit with a rock for a good while, just looking at its lines and spots, feeling it out, before she helps the image she sees there come out with her paints. She says the rocks feel lighter after she does that, and I have a feeling she probably feels lighter too.

Years ago, I found a small rock that looks exactly like a tiny foot. You can see the arch, the heel, and the ball of the foot clear as day. Sometimes I think it might be the petrified slipper that some mīmīkwīsiw left behind. I carry it in my bundle, and sometimes I'll take it out and just hold it for a while, feel its weight, run my thumb over its curves and edges. Even though I've looked at it a thousand times, if I pause to notice the colour, the coolness, the little specks in its surface, I usually find something new. My mind will wander;

then it'll come back to the tiny stone slipper. Holding it reminds me that paying attention to small things can bring a calm I often forget I have, especially when life feels unsettled.

Isaac said, "Open those flaps! Stop three times! Breathe! Focus on what's right here and right now. Maapii! Open the curtains and let the sunlight and all of those emotions pour in. Better yet, open the flaps of your deadly Indian wigwam and breathe it all in." Wherever you are, whatever is going on, this is a good reminder to pause and consciously let some fresh air and light into your space, both inside and out.

And it is true that just getting outside and connecting with Mother Earth is a powerful way to grow our present self and feel our place in the world, that true interconnected self. She gives us so many chances to ground ourselves if we pay attention to the cycles of life all around us. Making a habit of stepping outside each day, even for just a few minutes, helps us notice the small changes as the seasons turn, the way new life emerges in spring, the fullness of summer, the beauty of fall as things let go, and the stillness that winter invites. Watching how the animals and plants live, how they adapt and follow the natural cycles of their environment, can make us more aware of time and our own part in it all.

When we are stuck with difficult thoughts and feelings, burning our medicines can bring us to a different space. Vivian says that the point of smudging isn't to banish our difficult emotions. On a number of occasions, when someone in circle was struggling, I remember Vivian saying, "Don't interrupt their healing!" if anyone was rushing over to smudge them. Our medicines help clear away some of the fog that can obstruct our spirit's view so we can see our thoughts, feelings, and what our bodies are telling us with a little more clarity.

Finally, when we are feeling overwhelmed or cut off, remember the strength and healing that exists in community. Seeking out gatherings where experiences are shared with respect, participating with a kind heart, listening deeply, and offering your own voice when you feel ready—these are ways we discover a strength and resilience that we might have forgotten we had. These are simple ways of being that our cultures have held for us, invitations to connect and to learn how to carry our hearts gently in our walk with the other human and nonhuman spirits on this journey.

BRINGING IT HOME

Through our visits with Isaac and Vivian, we have tuned in to a version of self that is here now and connected to all Creation. Their teachings shine light on a path to embracing our present experiences, acknowledging our pain, and recognizing the interconnectivity that binds us all together. It's a lot to take in, but it's worth considering how these ideas might apply to our own lives.

For those of us who spend a lot of time worrying about the future or ruminating on the past (which I'm pretty sure is everyone), Isaac's teachings of being here now (maapii) offer a different way of engaging with our experiences. Vivian's perspective on our spiritual essence reminds us that we're more than the labels we've collected or the stories we tell about ourselves. This can be particularly powerful when we're grappling with self-criticism or decision-limiting beliefs.

For Indigenous readers dealing with intergenerational trauma or feeling disconnected from their culture, these teachings might offer some pathways for healing and reconnection. Practices like spending time on the land, engaging in Ceremony, or exploring your language—even in small ways—can be powerful tools for reclaiming identity and finding balance. If you've found yourself in relationship with depression or anxiety, you might find some solace in the idea of interconnectedness. Recognizing our place within the larger web of Creation can provide a sense of belonging and purpose, even in our darkest, most lonely moments. As you reflect on what you have read, consider how embracing our shared humanity and seeing our part in the natural world can lead to healing and wholeness. By recognizing the sacredness of each moment and our interconnectedness, we cultivate a sense of belonging and purpose, transcending beyond the isolating labels we've put upon ourselves.

In the coming days, maybe you will notice those moments when you're fully present, even if they are fleeting. How does it feel to really be aware of your connection to the world around you? How might you invite more of these moments into your life? Don't overcomplicate things. Where your feet are making contact with the ground, imagine drawing a little chalk outline around each one. Press your tongue to the roof of your mouth for a moment. Press your fingertips together for ten seconds.

Remember, we're not trying to achieve some idealized state of constant mindfulness. That's impossible. But just noticing those moments where our awareness has been carried off by the day-to-day distractions and struggles and bringing it back to our body and to the universe around us is possible. In fact, the most distracted among us (present company included) really have the most opportunities for mindful realignment. If you get distracted and come back to your body over and over, then you've flexed your mindfulness muscle over and over. A good workout.

We still have a ways to go, but hopefully this part of the journey has given you some good things for your bundle.

8.

DETOUR

All journeys have detours. Sometimes it's a little orange sign pointing the way off the beaten path for a stretch before the next sign leads you back to the open road; other times it's a twenty-foot sinkhole that swallows you whole. I fell through mine on a Thursday morning in February.

At 10:15 a.m. the phone rang with news that for years I had labelled irrational thought, while lying in bed trying to keep my heart from bursting out of my chest. The words from the phone said that my brother was dead, but their meaning got scrambled on the way from my ear to my temporal lobe. "Are you sure?" I think I said. For about two minutes after I hung up the phone, I sat and stared and felt nothing. A deep blank ocean of nothing. I used to think it was impossible to stop thinking completely; Lord knows I've tried a million times in vain to quiet my brain when it decides to rake me over the coals for my many sins. But for two long minutes, there was just the horrifying emptiness.

When the words finally landed, the air was sucked out of my lungs like an escape hatch blown out of a space shuttle. I leaned forward and put my head down to try to put the breath back in. I felt the pressure build up in my sinuses, but the tears didn't come. There was disbelief and denial, but I also immediately knew it was true. I remember being startled by the numbness. "Shouldn't I be crying?" I thought to myself. But I just sat there. I'm not sure how long this went on for. It felt like an eternity, but my best estimate now is maybe five or ten minutes. I still think about that moment and feel like I might somehow still be sitting there staring. Einstein was right.

Eventually, I managed to float up the stairs and knock on the door to Lisa's office. The door opened, and she smiled broadly and then froze. She could see the panic on my face. "Jerome died," I said. The moment the words left my mouth, the pressure behind my eyes finally burst, spilling out in parallel saltwater cascades. In the twenty years before this, I had cried only a handful of times. I made up for lost time for sure.

In my efforts to overcome generations of emotional suppression, grief has always been the last crusade. I have very slowly learned to sit with anger, anxiety, fear, and sadness. To look them in the eye and ask them what they are trying to tell me. Sometimes I still get caught up with them and let them take the wheel in my life briefly, but more and more often, I can pause and step back, see the thoughts and emotions as something I can hold gently, and remember that I have a choice about what to do next. Things that would have sent me into a fit of rage or had me pacing the floor with panic years ago now have less control over my actions. But grief is a different kind of animal; it doesn't negotiate, it doesn't sit still, it doesn't go gently. In the beginning, it doesn't even relent long enough for you to catch your breath.

Grief isn't an emotion. It's an endless collection of thoughts, images, memories, sensations, and emotions. An anger, anxiety, guilt, sadness, yearning, flashback sandwich. I felt all of these in the long drive to meet my family and collect my brother's things from his apartment. I felt all of these while seeing the grief on the faces of his children and my parents at his funeral. I felt all of these when I tied up prayer ties for his journey. And when I lit the fire and put out a feast plate on the first anniversary of his passing. I feel all of them now.

I had written the first part of this book before my brother started his journey to the spirit world, but afterwards I couldn't bring myself to type another word. The grief was washing over me in waves, pulling away for a period while I busied myself with work, rearranging my books, or building an unnecessary loft in the garage. But then a sound or smell, a song or picture, a word or look would signal the return of the tide. The stickiest thoughts and emotions are what I refer to as the guilt-and-shame tag-team partnership. Think the old '80s wrestlers who take turns tagging in so one can hold you while the other cracks a metal chair over your head or gives you a leg drop from the top ropes. I thought almost continuously about what I might have done to prevent my brother's death, all the things I should have done, the millions of possibilities that might have somehow changed fate. I spent hours fantasizing about it, and somehow it felt like a possibility, like it could still happen, like I could make a call or drive up there and everything would be reversed.

For a long time, I set this book aside. The thought of writing about wellness while incapacitated by grief felt hypocritical. I did eventually make it back here, but to be honest, as I sit here now, I don't know that the person who started this journey with you all those pages ago exists anymore. There is a part of me that is branded with the loss, which I am certain will carry the marking of pain and regret until it's my turn to travel home. But I am here now. Perhaps if I tell you what I saw on my journey off the beaten path, what helped and what hindered, it will help you with the detours you might take in your life.

They say hindsight is 20/20, but I'm not so sure. Plenty of times I've looked back and wondered what the hell happened and how. But in the year following my brother's passing, I found myself once again leaning into my culture and the science of psychological flexibility, or perhaps more accurately psychological flexibility through culture.

A few months after the funeral, I attended an Ancestor Ceremony at Six Nations of the Grand River at the lodge of Diane Longboat and Cynthia White, two Elders who have been kind guides on my journey of healing and learning while I've been far from my home territory. I have fasted out on their land many times; even in the dead of winter, they would set me up under their lodge between the sacred fire and a wood-burning stove that you had to keep roaring or you'd wake up frozen on the ground in your sleeping bag.

The fasts were always tough, but the Ancestor Ceremony was especially hard, as I had to hear my experience of grief reflected in the songs and prayers. It was excruciating to think of my brother as one of the ancestors rather than the flesh and blood that I had looked at with such intense admiration as a kid. He was captain of his hockey team and had a black leather jacket, muscles, and a thick head of '80s head-banger hair that made him seem larger than life to me. This is the image I still have of him in my head now.

Cynthia raised her pipe for my brother a few days after the Ceremony and gave me a teaching: "When we leave this body and pass through that western doorway on our journey home, we leave behind all of the debris we have collected along the way. The guilt and shame and fear don't come along with us, just that true part of us underneath it all. Our ancestors are waiting there for us, all of those that have gone on ahead are preparing a feast to welcome us back. But before all of that, we are greeted by all of the animals we have ever loved. That stray cat you fed as a kid, that baby bird you nursed back to health in a shoebox. And of course, all of the dogs that have given you their complete loyalty and friendship without expectation of anything in return. There they are, all their true unburdened selves as well; and they are so happy to see you."

Jerome's first dog, Max, was a massive Samoyed-Husky mix who would follow him everywhere. Legend has it that Jerome and his friends were playing on a construction site not far from the mine with Max keeping watch. While climbing some piece of equipment, Jerome fell and hit his head, knocking himself unconscious. The other kids surrounded him to see if he was okay, but Max sprinted into action snarling at the kids with teeth bare and tail straight. The neighbourhood kids of course ran at the sight of Max on guard, who proceeded to drag Jerome home by his sweater. Max gets bigger and bigger every time I hear this story.

Shaska was a less heroic dog that my brother had taken care of for a friend who had fallen on hard times. Shaska had obviously seen some stuff in her many dog years and was pretty sketchy and mangy looking. Jerome took to calling her Bitey McBiteBite after the infamous choking incident. Shaska had been chewing on a plastic bottle cap and got it lodged in her throat. Things were looking dire, until Jerome grabbed Shaska by the scruff, crammed a finger and thumb down her throat, and dislodged the cap. Shaska thanked Jerome by leaving a bite that would require sixteen stitches and a tetanus booster. Hence the new moniker: Bitey. She would completely lose it when she spotted a housefly, snapping at the air wildly while spinning in circles and knocking things over. Jerome could yell, "Git the fly, boy!" in a pronounced Appalachian backwoods accent and send Shaska/Bitey into a frenzy of spinning and snapping and barking even if there wasn't actually a fly. Jerome would howl with laughter at the chaos.

The thought of my brother being greeted by the many dogs he had loved over the years brought me brief moments of peace during those first few weeks when the grief was thick. I am extremely thankful for that teaching and the moments it offered.

The Sun Dance that summer was difficult. Not because of the thirst or hunger, the physical pain or fatigue. It was the rawness with which I was forced to confront the grief. No distractions in the big lodge out in the bush. No cell phone for doomscrolling endless stupid videos, no junk food to cram into my face, no shows to binge-watch until 3:00 a.m., no articles to read, no emails to send, no papers to write. Just me, my grief, and the tree.

My mom was there as a dancer (she has danced for almost twenty years straight accompanying my other siblings on their four-year commitments), and I saw the grief surrounding her like a dark cloud too. I also saw grief following the other dancers, the helpers, and the community members who had lost loved ones and who were currently losing loved ones, many of whom had lost more than most could ever comprehend. It was all out in the open, not hidden away behind closed doors with a stiff upper lip the way we are taught to handle things today. Death, condolences, funeral, and then back to work; that's grief in the West. And if you dare to grieve too long (more than twelve months, says the American Psychological Association), you might just end up in a Naming Ceremony. Prolonged grief disorder, they will call you. A'ho!

I once heard an Elder say that to grieve for someone is our kinship responsibility. After they go, we hold their memory in our hearts. And when they leave us early, we commit to having the experiences they will have missed, so that they can live those through us. To think of grief as a responsibility rather than a curse is a very different perspective. That part of me that is branded with the loss of my brother is also the part that holds and loves him today. In that case, I am proud to bare those scars and look forward to doing so as long as I am on this earth.

9.

THE FIRST WAVES OF GRIEF

As Jerome made his way to the spirit world, the urge to escape gripped me like a vise. The allure of withdrawing from everyone around me, numbing the pain with booze or pills or rage or sleep was almost irresistible. Behind the sorrow, I seethed with anger. I started a list in my head of all the people who might even be remotely responsible and fantasized about elaborate revenge scenarios. I wanted to lash out at others. I wanted to lash out at myself. The pressure was steadily building, and I felt I might soon pop.

But grief, like water, eventually erodes any container. Water finds a way around any barrier. Water will humble the mightiest rock faces into smooth plateaus. One of the things I've learned, and continue to learn, is that grief will leak out of you and back into the world where it belongs, but this can be an excruciatingly slow process, maybe letting out only a few drops every now and then, or it might come in bursts of relief followed by periods of painful holding, or as a steady flow that becomes your new normal and you don't even notice it anymore.

Grief will leak out of you, fast or slow; the choice is yours.

Len's description of pain as natural, intimate, and fluid took on new meaning while I visited with grief. Grief flows through life, sometimes overwhelming you like a tsunami, other times a quiet stream, but it is never still. I thought of this when the grief came in waves. I think I expected it to be super intense at the beginning and then slowly taper off into something manageable later on. But it hasn't happened that way. It comes in like a hurricane and then leaves for a period before returning to throw things around again. The down period could be a few hours, a few days, maybe even a week without the storm descending, but it always comes back.

Likely as a product of wanting to hide my pain from others, whether from embarrassment or an urge not to burden my family, I took to scheduling my visits with grief in isolation. Usually late at night, after everyone had gone to sleep and I could hear the chorus of snoring around the house, I would sit in the bathroom, or in my office, or at the end of the bed, and sob. Sometimes I would stare at Jerome's picture or one of the things that he had left behind or something that reminded me of him, and just let the grief in and out completely. Afterwards, I would feel a sense of relief; other times I would feel completely depleted and need to lie down. But in all these moments of grief, I was there with the painful thoughts, memories, sensations, and emotions in an undefended way.

The painful experiences came and they went, and in between there were pleasant memories where I would chuckle to myself before sobbing again. I didn't know it at the time, but this openness changed my relationship with grief greatly. Slowly, I have begun to see the thoughts as thoughts, feel the feelings as feelings, and view the memories as memories. The difference between this and the mindless grief I experienced early on and outside of these moments is that often the thoughts or memories that snuck up randomly at the store or while sitting at my desk would pull me down into those green, weedy depths as I kicked away frantically trying to fight them off. Of course, as Grandmother Renée shared, this just left me more and more tangled in the difficult experiences and the stories they told about me.

While it is still painful, I have found that the intermittent release of these purposeful moments has facilitated a relationship with grief that is less battle and more partnership. More of a "Hey, Grief, how can we get through this together?" than an "I wish you would leave me the hell alone!"

We have been told for a long time that there is an appropriate and stepwise way to grieve. First we are supposed to enter the *denial stage*. It didn't happen, it's not real, we are not affected by it because it can't be true. With this comes feelings of shock and numbness. The reality of loss is incomprehensible, and the mind struggles to accept this new, painful truth.

Next we transition on to the *anger stage*, where we rage against the perceived injustice of the loss. The turmoil and conflict here is both internal and external, the loss is unfair and we are overcome by frustration. Here we lash out at ourselves and at those around us.

Then we are supposed to find ourselves in the *bargaining stage*, where we are bombarded with "if only" thoughts while we try to negotiate away the pain and fantasize about scenarios where the outcome is different. What if they got better, what if they reached out for help, what if I was there just in time, what if they were still here?

As the temporary relief provided by the bargaining stage fades, the intense reality of the loss sets in, leading to a period of crushing sadness and the *depression stage*. Here we experience the complete deep sorrow of the loss in our bodies, minds, hearts, and souls.

In the fifth and final stage of *acceptance*, we gradually acknowledge the reality of the situation and begin to find ways to learn to live with it. This doesn't necessarily mean we are happy and everything goes back to normal or we forget; it means we learn to live our lives with the reality of the loss.

While I can certainly relate to all five stages, as I'm sure those of you who are grieving can, it isn't quite this neat and organized, is it? During the first year, I'm certain I went through all five stages in a completely randomized order almost every day. It was like spinning the wheel of grief. There would be days after acknowledging what had happened and being inconsolable that I would suddenly be struck with the possibility that it wasn't true at all, that I could call him right then and he would answer. Then I would be overcome with anger and regret. Back to depression, then to denial and bargaining. I was bouncing around these grief stages like a pinball. Grief is not a straightforward or linear journey through stages. We move between experiences in a nonsequential way, and even experience multiple components of these stages simultaneously. The five stages of grief model is devoid of any cultural consideration and built for WEIRD (Western, educated, industrialized, rich, and democratic) audiences, which we know can have disastrous effects when applied to diverse populations without the appropriate considerations.

But to be fair to Elisabeth Kübler-Ross who wrote the book *On Death and Dying* and originally developed the five stages of grief model back in 1969, much progress has been made since this linear and systematic perspective was developed. Most models on grief and loss now acknowledge the dynamic and culture-bound nature of grief. That said, the five-stages model has dominated public discourse on grief through pop psychology and media for decades. And it is still the first thing that pops up when you look for information on grief.

Does recovering from grief mean being back to normal? Does it mean being happy again? Does it mean forgetting about all the pain of that loss? Does it mean moving on? If so, I don't want it. If someone said I could relinquish all of the sorrow, guilt, regret, anger, and anxiety but it would mean letting go of my brother's memory, I would punt that genie's lamp into the nearest pond or river without a second thought. Recovery means changing our relationship with the loss, learning to feel the pain as a reminder of the love we had and still have for that person. We recover when we allow the pain of loss to warm rather than freeze us. It hurts because it matters. It hurts because he matters. It hurts because I love him.

The truth is that grief is normal. And however you grieve is normal. Even in the chaos of calms and storms, it is the normal response to loss. Too often our mind tells us, "You're grieving wrong! You shouldn't be feeling that! You shouldn't be thinking that! You should be thinking and feeling this instead! How come you're not going through the five stages like everyone else? Where's the denial? Where's the anger? You can't even get grief right!" And of course that leads to all sorts of self-stories. Is there something wrong with me? Am I a heartless monster who feels nothing? Am I overreacting?

Len's teaching on being mindful of our minds' tendency towards labelling and dualistic thinking (good/bad, right/wrong) can be especially useful when our inner critic shows up to kick our butts with guilt and regret. Grief blurs the lines of good and bad, right and wrong. Even our most painful experiences have purpose and are likely an integral part of our life's narrative. If we can see grief as a complex and integrative experience, we can let it do its work. The alternative is rarely productive. Grief, much like the wind, is a force that can topple us if we stand rigid against it. But we can bend and sway with these gusts of emotion, not to dodge the pain but to let it pass through our branches with grace and kindness.

One of the stickiest experiences for me in all of this has been guilt. As a health care provider, a mental health professional, and a brother, how could I have let this happen? What could I have done that would have prevented his death? If I had visited or called sooner or more often, would things have been different?

About a week after my brother passed, I had a dream indistinguishable from waking life. We are sitting at an empty table at the POW pub. The entire bar is empty, the lights are on, and there is no music playing. No hustle and bustle of the weird and wonderful regulars the way there had been years before. I can smell the musty smell of pool tables with too many drinks poured on them over too many years. Elvis, Marilyn, and an assortment of hockey players decorate nicotine-yellowed wood panel walls. The vinyl floors have seen better days, with scuff marks that tell the tale of so many a last-call boogie. Jerome looks good. He is healthy, fit, and content. He smiles at me and doesn't say a word. I do all the talking. I list all the ways he could still be alive. All the things I could have done that might have changed the way things are. All the possibilities that would make the horrible truth untrue. I am pleading and arguing and trying my best to persuade. With each good point I make, Jerome just nods in acknowledgement, still smiling, but not looking terribly concerned. He doesn't seem worried at all, he doesn't look afraid, upset, or alone. I woke up as it seemed he might open his mouth to say something. I cried hard for about an hour and lay in bed for the rest of the day thinking about that dream.

Guilt is a familiar companion on the journey of grief, one that can take many forms and wear many masks. It's that nagging feeling that we could have done more, been better, or somehow prevented the inevitable. Guilt in grief is complex, part emotion and part thought process, often rooted in our deepest fears and unrealistic expectations. It's the voice that whispers, "If only" and "What if," keeping us tethered to the past when we need to move forward.

This guilt can be rational, stemming from real mistakes or regrets, or completely irrational, born from our need to make sense of the senseless. It's a tricky illusion of control in a situation where we often feel powerless. While guilt is a common passenger on the grief train, it's not an inevitable one, and its presence and intensity can vary widely from person to person. Understanding guilt—its origins, its purpose, and its impact—is a crucial step in navigating the choppy waters of loss and finding a way to shore.

Guilt is a chameleon in the world of grief, changing its colours and intensity as we move through our journey of loss. It's not a one-size-fits-all experience; rather, it's as unique as our fingerprints, shaped by our personal histories, cultural backgrounds, and the nature of our loss. Some of us might feel crushed by the weight of survivor's guilt, while others grapple with the gnawing feeling of not having done enough.

The trick is to recognize our own particular flavour of guilt without judgment, understanding that it's a common part of the grieving process. It's also crucial to remember that guilt isn't a static emotion. It ebbs and flows, sometimes hitting us like a sonic boom, other times receding to a whisper. This fluctuation doesn't mean we're grieving "wrong"—there's no such thing. Instead, it's part of the messy, nonlinear path of healing.

Guilt can be a sneaky character in our grief story, often masquerading as a way to make sense of our loss. It tricks us into thinking that if we feel bad enough, somehow we can turn back time or make amends for perceived wrongs. But here's the kicker: While guilt might feel like it's helping us process our grief, it can actually keep us stuck, ruminating on the past instead of adjusting to our new reality.

That said, guilt isn't always the villain. Sometimes, it can be a catalyst for transformation. By examining our guilt—its roots, its validity, its purpose—we can use it as a springboard for personal growth or meaningful action. Maybe that guilt over not spending enough time with a loved one becomes the motivation to strengthen our connections with those still with us. Or perhaps the guilt over unresolved conflicts becomes the impetus to practise forgiveness—of others and ourselves. Self-compassion is our strongest ally in this struggle. Why can't we treat ourselves with the same kindness we'd offer a grieving friend? Of course, this doesn't mean letting ourselves off the hook for real mistakes, but rather acknowledging our humanity—our limitations, our imperfections, and, yes, our capacity for growth and change.

Talking about guilt can feel like opening Pandora's box, but sharing these feelings with trusted others can be incredibly healing. It allows us to voice those fears and regrets and, often, to hear perspectives that challenge our guilt-ridden narrative. And many times, we'll find that our loved ones are carrying their own guilt stories, which from our vantage point may seem completely irrational or may have part-truths weighted heavily by the emotional baggage of the loss. This might give us an opportunity for some perspective taking and to reflect on our own experience of guilt as just that, an experience. Of course, this isn't always easy—guilt can be an extremely private, sometimes shameful feeling. But in bringing it to light, we often find that we're not alone in our experiences.

As we work through guilt in bereavement, it's important to keep an eye out for warning signs that it's become excessive or harmful. If guilt is preventing us from taking care of our basic needs, isolating us from others, or leading to thoughts of self-harm, it's time to seek help. Remember, asking for help isn't a sign of weakness—it's a courageous step towards healing. We heal together, never alone, after all.

In the end, dealing with guilt in grief is about finding balance. It's acknowledging the feeling without letting it consume us, using it as a tool for growth when appropriate, and knowing when to let it go. Often the recipe requires forgiveness—of others, of circumstances beyond our control, and, most importantly, of ourselves. Self-compassion can serve as a compass that guides us back to the path of healing when we lose our way.

MINDFULNESS PUSH-UPS

An Elder once told me that when their heart starts to fill with the heaviness of grief, anger, or sadness, they take a quiet moment to sit with both the good and the hard that life has handed them. They'll start with a memory that brings warmth, a pleasant memory of a time of love and connection or just feeling alive. They notice the colour of the sky in that memory, the sound of laughter, how their posture looked, what they were wearing, what the space around them looked like, and then they let themselves linger there for a while. After that they would try to sit with a more difficult experience. A thought or memory that keeps coming back. As before, they make the experience as vivid as possible. They notice how their body reacts, where it tenses, and they name it gently, the way they might greet a relative at the door. Back and forth between the two experiences they will jump, training their mind to always come back to their body and the world around them.

10.

A SPACE BETWEEN THE WAVES

In grief, my mind often leaps between the past and the future, revisiting moments with my brother or imagining what life will look like without him here. Sometimes those memories bring comfort. Other times they stir up regret and longing. At their worst, they can pull me so far from the present that I forget where I am.

Isaac's teaching about maapii, being here now, has been a lifeline in those moments. To be here now means being willing to sit with grief rather than to push it away, and to notice it without being consumed. I feel this most clearly in small, purposeful moments, like when I have held Jerome's picture or listened to a song he loved. In those moments I am just there with the spirit of my sadness, noticing the thoughts that come and go, feeling the weight in my chest, letting the tears come when they want to.

The more I practise, the more I begin to see grief as something with its own tides. Sometimes it crashes over me like storm waves. Other times it laps gently at the edges of my day. Like Vivian's teaching about water, grief changes form. It is always moving. And in that movement, there are spaces, brief moments when the waves pull back and I can catch my breath.

Even in the hardest times, I can sense a part of me that is watching from a place of spirit. Western practitioners might call it dissociation, but it feels like something else entirely, an awareness that can see my human experience without being swept away. In those moments, I remember that I am not my grief. I am in relationship with grief.

This awareness also helps me catch the stories my mind tells about how I should be grieving. Stories like "you should be stronger than this" or "you will never be happy again." They come often, and they sound convincing. But when I see them as thoughts instead of truths, they loosen their grip.

On many occasions I have taken my bundle and sat on the rocks by the river, offering prayers for my brother and listening to the water rush past. Sometimes the grief is loud, and still, I notice other things: the warmth of the sun on my face, the songs of all sorts of birds, the smell of the water or my medicines burning. These things do not erase the pain; they sit alongside it, reminding me that life is still happening and that my brother is still part of it.

Over time, I've started noticing how often grief pulls me into autopilot. Sometimes I get to the end of the day without remembering much of it. Little by little I have been working on orienting more to simple tasks, such as walking up the stairs or washing the dishes. They seem insignificant, but they are a lifeline in the face of sometimes overwhelming memory and emotion. Bringing awareness to grief doesn't require that we "figure it out" or make it smaller. Awareness allows our difficult experiences to exist without letting them take everything.

Vivian once told me, "Grief is a heart wound, and when we work to fix it with our minds, we fall short. Only a heart can fix a heart." Her words remind me that presence is not intended to be an escape from pain. It's more like honouring what we've lost without losing sight of the life and love that are still here.

Grief travels through the whole of us. It shows itself in the body, in the heart, in the mind, and in the spirit. Sometimes it is a heaviness in the chest, a lump in the throat, or an ache in the limbs. Sometimes it is a bolt of anger or sadness, or a thick fog of numbness. Sometimes it is a mind full of memories and questions. These parts move together, shaping and reshaping how we experience our loss. Yet in grief, we often focus on only one or two of these places and lose touch with the others. In those challenging moments, making space to notice each part can feel like gathering scattered pieces of ourselves.

There is no single way to grieve. Some days awareness will feel like an anchor. Other days you will need other kinds of support. However you meet your grief, meet it gently. Notice the thoughts that arise, the emotions that pass through, the sensations in your body. Remember that you are more than your grief. You are the one who sees it, feels it, and lives through it. Awareness will not take the pain away, but it may give you a place to stand as the waves come in and out.

ON THE ROAD AGAIN

The road does not look the same as it did. Every mile forward takes me farther from the place where I had last seen my brother. Grief is in the passenger seat now, changing the way the gravel sounds underneath the tires and how the treetops seem to chase the car. I thought about turning back and about just pulling over and never moving again, but I know there are teachings I have yet to hear. The next part of the trip takes me to Ron Linklater and Gloria Oshkabewisens-McGregor. I know they will have things to say about the joy of being alive and the sharp ache of loss. Maybe those teachings will meet me where I am, right in the middle of it all. So I'll keep going for a bit and see what happens.

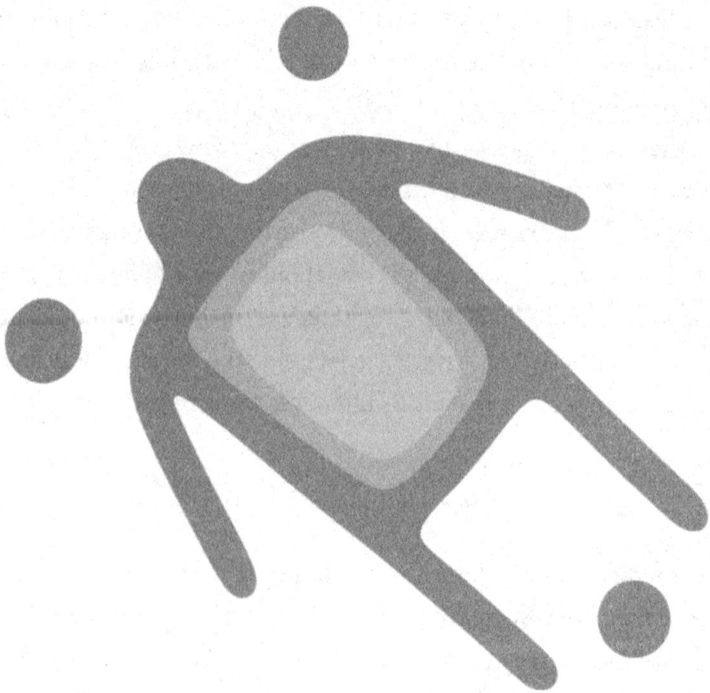

MITHO-TŌTAMOWIN

Maybe you were never taught how to carry that heavy load on your mind, but certainly you have been taught to move, you have been taught to reach. You're the only one who can start to reach.

Gloria Oshkabewisens-McGregor

11.

MITHO-TŌTAMOWIN

The Cree word *mitho-tōtamowin* carries a teaching about how we are in our worlds. *Mitho* means "good or right," and *itōtamowin* speaks to the act of doing, of carrying something out. When you put them together, the word points us towards something essential—purposeful action. It's a reminder about living in a way that reflects what we value, what we're responsible for, and the kind of life we want to be able to look back on without regret.

When we live engaged with what matters, we shape a life through repeated choices. Not dramatic ones, most of the time. Ordinary ones, made again and again. Over time, those choices leave a mark. You begin to recognize it in people you meet. There is a sense that they know what they are answerable to. They are not flawless or free from struggle. They falter like the rest of us. But they continue to act from love, loyalty, respect, responsibility, family, and community. Even when loss and crisis keep returning, they remain involved in their lives and in the lives of others. They keep doing and being. I'm sure if you think for a moment you can bring one of these people to the forefront of your mind.

Before we can live well, before anything else, really, we need values clarity. We need to know what we want to stand for in this one life we've been given.

WHAT MATTERS MOST?

Often when something hurts, it is because there is something important in that moment. The sharpness of anxiety before a conversation, the heaviness after being seen, or the dread before entering a room can point towards longing: a wish to belong, to be understood, to connect. When the mind brings stories of failure or self-doubt, it may be showing where our care is strongest. Pain and value are often bound together.

Pause and notice what matters to you right now. It might be a person you care about, a responsibility you hold, or a place that has shaped you. It might be family, community, or the land you live on. It might be someone who is no longer here. What matters is usually close, even when it is hard to put into words. Alongside these longings, other experiences show up as well: thoughts of not being enough, shame, old memories, the ache of grief. They pull at our attention when we forget they are only part of the picture.

Caught in these stories, we often move away from what matters. We hide, shut down, or numb. These strategies can soften the moment, yet over time they widen the distance from the life we want. The invitation is to notice and ask, What small step might we take towards what matters, even with these feelings here?

To be engaged is to recognize this tenderness and walk with it. It is living in alignment with our values and showing up in ways that reflect who we are becoming. Acting good means tending the places we inhabit, the people we walk with, and the teachings we carry. It transforms attention into action. Everyday gestures can be powerful. Washing dishes can be care. Speaking clearly about what we need from others can be healing. Saying yes, saying no, resting, sharing food, breathing on the land, each can be a thread added to a meaningful life.

Even in pain, we continue to act. Each choice towards what matters is part of how a good life is made.

12.

RON LINKLATER

Our next stop brings us to the family camp of Ron Linklater, south of Saskatoon, Saskatchewan. Ron doesn't like being called an Elder, but people refer to him this way anyway because of his gentle approach, his immense knowledge, and his willingness to share it. Ron's father is the late Walter Linklater from the Anishinaabe community of Couchiching First Nation and his mother is Maria Linklater from Thunderchild Cree Nation. This gives Ron the unique position of carrying Anishinaabe and nēhiyawak teachings.

The Linklater family is a powerhouse. Walter was a legendary figure in his own right—a widely respected Elder who dedicated decades to teaching First Nations history and culture, advising governments, and overcoming many challenges to become a beacon of wisdom and guidance for his community. Maria has been a tireless advocate for Indigenous children and has fostered more than four hundred kids. In the 1970s she fought in court to prevent children with neurodevelopmental differences from being removed from their communities. Today, at eighty-five, Maria continues her important work as an Elder, advocate, and family matriarch. And the apple doesn't fall far from the tree. Ron's life has also been characterized by a commitment to serving others.

Ron grew up in Thunder Bay and, as a teenager, struggled with the impacts of intergenerational trauma handed down from the residential schools his parents attended. Ron would wrestle with anger, depression, and substance abuse as a young man; conditions that he says were rampant in his community. Ron's life would take a drastic turn, however, which he attributes to the support of two men who saw something in him and introduced him to the concept of the Red Road. Under their guidance, Ron experienced a spiritual transformation, overcoming his substance use challenges and finding stability and balance in his life.

Ron's journey led him to work extensively with the National Native Alcohol and Drug Abuse Program, where he walked alongside those seeking relief from generations of suffering. Although Ron is technically retired, he hasn't slowed down much. He teaches courses at the University of Manitoba, consults to hospitals, trains Indigenous organizations in traditional leadership, and regularly attends Ceremony. And if there is any time left over, he's out on the ice playing hockey or swinging a golf club somewhere warm.

Over the last number of years, I have had the privilege of listening to many of Ron's teachings. Ron's journey is a testament to survivance. "Both of my parents attended residential school," he shares. "The people who attended those schools wanted to give their children things like the language, Ceremony, or the ability to hunt and be on the land, but weren't able to. Maybe it was too painful, or maybe they were afraid their children would be punished as they had been. They couldn't pass those things down, and that caused many to lose themselves."

It's important to remember how recent this is. Ron often says, "History is now." We're not talking about ancient times, but about our parents, aunties, uncles, and grandparents. It's likely that some of you reading these words will have attended residential or day school. The wounds are still fresh, the impacts still reverberating through our communities like bone that aches when the weather changes.

Despite this, Ron's message isn't one of defeat. He never takes a deficit-based perspective. "Why, in spite of everything that has occurred to us, are we still able to be here and share the beauty of our culture with other nations?" he asks.

Ron believes that the persistence of Indigenous Peoples in the face of such adversity can be credited to our values. "Our values are inseparable from our kinship systems. Our grandparents and grandchildren, our aunties and uncles. Values are ultimately about family," he says. It's a stark contrast to the individualistic worldview that dominates much of modern society. Here, our values are not just personal preferences, but ties that bind us to our relatives, our ancestors, and the generations yet to come. "Our language and worldview contain a blueprint for living," he explains. "It constantly reminds us that we are connected to each other and with all of Creation." Even if we don't speak the language fluently, he insists, we can still embody its values through our actions, through how we treat each other and the world around us.

I've heard people speak of the seven generations teaching before, and I think many people will recognize it as something like "act in a way that will positively impact the seven generations that follow you," but the teaching is much more complex than this. As he holds out his hands to count his fingers, Ron says the seven generations teaching is a way of thinking that places us in the middle of a long line of ancestors and descendants. "One way of looking at this teaching is to see ourselves as one generation, one that has parents, grandparents, and great-grandparents. And if we go the opposite direction, we may have children, grandchildren, and if we are lucky, perhaps we will meet our great-grandchildren."

Ron shares a memory of his great-grandmother. "She was born in 1885. Her name was White Cap, but I called her cāpān," he says. *Cāpān* (pronounced cha-pan) is a nēhiyawīwin word that is used interchangeably to mean both great-grandparent and great-grandchild. "And she called me cāpān too; that's the great reciprocity of our language," Ron says.

The word itself reveals something incredible about the importance of Indigenous languages in the conceptualization of time, space, and the meaning of self. A similar word *nitāniskocāpān*, which speaks to even more distant relationships, contains morphemes that speak to an inextricable link. For example, the morpheme *anisko* ("following along, in sequence, joining one another") modifies the words for "pulls towards, draws towards him/herself" to become *āniskohpitam* ("lengthening by tying end-to-end"). When used in the context of the relationship between a great-grandchild and a great-grandparent, the word *nitāniskocāpān* may be best conceptualized as saying, "I pull myself towards you through time, extending myself so that we are one." So in a way, when Ron and his great-grandmother greeted each other with *cāpān*, they were really saying, "I am you."

Ron recalls cāpān's kindness, the softness of her hands on his face, her stories and laughter. He remembers struggling to pull at a plant while picking medicines with his mother and cāpān when he was maybe four years old. He heaved and heaved until the plant, root and all, came flying out of the ground, sending little Ron tumbling backwards onto his butt in the wet muskeg. Cāpān threw her head back with a great laugh and said in nēhiyawīwin, "This one will have great medicine one day." I think she was right about this, and I appreciate that I've had the opportunity to see and hear some of that medicine at work.

It is clear that Ron is truly grateful for the brief time he got to spend with his great-grandmother. "She was able to travel back into her past and bring those teachings forward to me." There's something beautiful in this image—the idea of teachings travelling across generations, expressed in the gentle touch of a great-grandmother's hand.

"Have you heard of John Herrington?" Ron says, moving seamlessly from one story to the next. I've heard this one before, but I love hearing it, so I lean in to listen once more. "John Harrington is Chickasaw. Just like me, he grew up watching those Apollo space missions on TV. Can you imagine? A young Indigenous kid, sitting in a cardboard box, pretending he's flying to the moon? Back then, for us, that kind of dream seemed about as likely as growing wings and flying there ourselves. But John had something special. He joined the navy, became a test pilot. Every step of the way, he was learning, growing, pushing himself. I'm sure it wasn't easy. Our people faced many barriers. John Herrington had to overcome obstacles along the way. But then in 1996, would you believe it, NASA chose him to be an astronaut. Six years later, there he was, strapped into the space shuttle *Endeavour*, about to blast off into space. Imagine that moment, all those years of dreaming, all that hard work, and now he's lying there, waiting for launch, realizing he's actually going to space."

John took his culture with him when he left earth. He took a Chickasaw flag, an eagle feather, and a traditional flute with him into space. With the flag, maybe John was saying, "I'm a Chickasaw astronaut. I carry my people with me."

Then there's the eagle feather. In our teachings, the eagle is sacred. It flies higher than any other bird, closer to the Creator. We use eagle feathers in our most important ceremonies. They represent wisdom, strength, and spiritual connection. They carry our prayers. By taking that feather into space, John was bringing the prayers and strength of his people with him. He was saying, "Even up here, among the stars, my ancestors are with me. "

Music is one of the ways we pass down our stories, our teachings. It's how we connect with the spirit world. By bringing that flute, John was carrying the voice of his people into space. Can you imagine the power of those traditional songs floating through the space station?

These items are symbols and a way of living our values, of staying true to who we are no matter where we go. John could have left all that behind. He chose to bring his whole self on that journey. Living well means achieving goals and doing it in a way that honours your values, your ancestors, your people and teachings. John's story reminds us that we can do great things, incredible things, while staying ourselves. We can reach for the stars and still keep our feet on the ground. Those sacred items he took with him? They're a reminder that our culture, our values, they lift us up, they help us achieve our dreams while staying true to who we are. That's the way of our ancestors, and that's the path we need to walk for the next seven generations.

Ron sits back with his warm signature smile. "That's the kind of story that gives me hope, baakozhendam."

THE SEVEN GRANDFATHERS

A foundational teaching of the Anishinaabe and nēhiyaw, and many other nations on Turtle Island, is that of the Seven Grandfathers or the Seven Sacred Teachings. Ron insists that the Grandfather teachings sit at the heart of an Anishinaabe understanding of values. Importantly, these teachings cannot be fully captured in the pages of a book. In our way, it could take many days for an Elder who carries them to tell the whole story, and then years of living and learning to truly grasp their meaning. What you read here can only offer a foundation for understanding collectivist values that might guide your own journey.

My understanding has been informed by James Vukelich Kaagegaabaw's writing on *The Seven Generations and the Seven Grandfather Teachings*. You may find it helpful also. But most important, if you find yourself drawn to these teachings, seek out a Knowledge Keeper who is willing to share them with you, offer tobacco, and engage as a learner in a good way.

Truth, Ron explains, is a way of living. In Anishinaabemowin, the word for "heart," *ode*, is also found in the word for "tongue," *odenaan*. This reminds us that truth involves speaking from the heart, living in alignment with your spirit, and honouring who you are. "I remember learning about our ceremonial Pipe, what we call ospwākan," Ron says. "It is a physical embodiment of our teaching about truth. The Pipe has two main parts: a stone bowl and a wooden stem. That wooden stem comes from trees that grow tall and straight. When we hold that Pipe, we are holding truth and faith in our hands. It is a powerful reminder to be like those trees, to stand tall and straight in our truth. Our ancestors kept our truths alive at great risk. They passed down our stories, our languages, our ways of being, even when it was dangerous to do so. Even when they were threatened with imprisonment and starvation. That is living in truth."

Honesty is closely connected to truth, but may focus more on specific actions and words in daily life. When we are in the Sweat Lodge or during a Pipe Ceremony, we are called to be honest with ourselves, others, and the Spirits. We cannot hide anything there. When we fast, when we pray, we are forced to confront ourselves honestly. When a person admits to making a mistake that affected others, despite feeling embarrassed, they clearly explain what happened, take responsibility for their actions, and offer to make amends. This act of honesty, being straightforward and truthful in a specific context, allows for resolution and maintains trust within the community.

After my brother died, I realized how often I dodged certain conversations or hid the heaviness I was carrying. Honesty for me became speaking plainly about my loss, admitting when I needed help, and resisting the urge to soften my truth just to make others more comfortable.

"In our language, we have a word, *gidizimagazimiis*," Ron explains. "It describes a state of being pitiful. You might think being pitiful is a bad thing, but there is wisdom in recognizing our limitations. Our ancestors understood that we are pitiful beings. We do not have the armour of the turtle or the strength of the bear. When we acknowledge that, we begin to call out for healing. We reconnect with the land, with Ceremony, with our true selves." There is power in that. It is like when we use tobacco in our ceremonies. We bring this small amount, this medicine, and it is like we are saying, "We are pitiful beings. We need help." That is how we become well again.

Think about the tobacco seed. It is tiny, barely visible. You might look at it and think, "This will never amount to anything." But we nurture it, we talk to it, we give it water and attention. From that tiny, seemingly insignificant seed, a sacred plant grows tall, with great broad leaves and the ability to carry our prayers. Anytime your ego is getting the better of you, things are going to your head, maybe you start feeling like you are really wise, great, strong, and powerful, go out West and find one of those great red cedars and try to push it around a bit and see how powerful you feel then.

Loss has made it harder to pretend I can do everything on my own. I am learning to accept help without shame, to admit what I do not know, and to see myself as part of a wider circle that includes those who have grieved before me and those who will grieve after.

Respect is acknowledging the sanctity of the life around you. We recognize that everything has a spirit and a purpose. Our language itself teaches us respect. "When we use words like *Gizhemanidoo* for Creator, or when we refer to the rocks as Grandfathers, we are showing respect by acknowledging their spiritual nature and importance," Ron says. "I remember as a young boy, when I was picking medicines with my great-grandmother. She taught me to approach the plants with respect and awareness, to offer tobacco and give thanks, to take only what we needed. In our way, we see ourselves as part of Creation. The trees, the animals, the rocks and water, they are all our relatives." When you speak of everything being alive and having spirit, and being related to you, you treat everything with respect. Respecting grief and hurt may mean allowing it to move in its own time, offering ourselves patience, and treating my own process with the same care I would give another who was mourning.

Love is one of our most sacred teachings. We experience this love in Ceremony. Our language carries it too. When we use words like *niijaanis* for our children or *nimaamaa* for our mothers, we are expressing that deep connection of love. "I remember as a child, my mother would hold my baby siblings and ask, 'Awin ababii nso?—

'Whose baby are you?' And they would reply, 'Nimaamaa.' That simple exchange was full of love," Ron shares.

Love is also about how we connect with the land and all living things. It shows up in generosity, kindness, and care for others. It is also about healing. When we embrace our teachings, when we go to Ceremony, when we speak our language, these acts of love help us heal from the traumas we carry. When we live with love, we are living the way Creator intended us to live.

In the months after my brother's passing, love often showed up in small and practical ways. It was sending and receiving a short message, making food, or sitting with someone without much to say. When I could not be present in person or make a call just yet, it meant holding people in mind and not turning away. It meant staying connected in the ways I could, I guess.

Courage is about having a strong heart. This is a spiritual kind of strength. In our history, we have faced tremendous challenges. "For over five hundred years, our people have endured repeated attempts to destroy our culture, languages, ceremonies, and our bodies. But we are still here." Ron shares, "That is the courage to keep going, to hold on to our ways even when it was hard. I think about my cāpān, my great-grandmother. She was born in 1885, the same year the government outlawed our Sun Dance Ceremony. Can you imagine the courage it took for her generation to keep our teachings alive when people were being starved or thrown into jail for it? They had to be strong-hearted to pass on our stories, our languages, our ceremonies in secret. They took action to keep those traditions alive in spite of the risks.

"It also takes courage to heal. We carry wounds from the past, from residential schools, from being taken from our families, from being told our ways are wrong or evil. It takes great courage to face that pain, to hold it gently, reclaim our true identities. I remember when I first started going to ceremonies as a young man. It was scary. I did not know the language. I did not know the protocols. But I had to find the courage in my heart to keep going, to keep learning. It takes a lot of courage to be kind, to be generous, to forgive." Courage means doing what is right even when you are afraid, especially when you are afraid.

Wisdom is about seeing the big picture and understanding the connections between all things. Wisdom is about seeing the world clearly. "The word *kīhci-wāpātamowin* can be translated as 'a big look,' about seeing all of the context in something and understanding that it is inseparable from the rest of Creation, including you," Ron says. It is a spiritual way of looking with great vision.

Wisdom is also knowing how to use the other teachings: love, respect, honesty, courage, humility, truth. You find wisdom through experience, from living the teachings day after day. All the teachings are connected. "They are all part of what we call *mino bimaadiziwin*, living the good life," Ron says. When we live by these teachings, we are healing ourselves, our families, our communities, our nation, and the earth itself. That is the power of these teachings. That is why they have been passed down for so many generations, and why it is so important that we keep passing them on.

WHEN VALUES CONFLICT

Ron says that becoming clear on our values can be tough these days. There are many things that are valuable to us, and from time to time, those things don't jibe well with one another. Ron told me a story about a friend who worked in the mines in Northern Manitoba when they were both younger men.

The job paid well and provided his friend with a level of security and freedom that were really important to him, but he was intimately aware of the damage that the mining companies were doing to the land and how the environmental harm was impacting his relatives. In my own hometown in Northern Manitoba, the closing of the mine led to a complete collapse of the local economy, which resembles something of a ghost town now.

The extraction of zinc, gold, silver, pyrite, and cadmium made a number of shareholders extremely rich in the 1980s, but very little of that wealth made its way into the community, where Indigenous Peoples continue to live in third-world conditions. In addition to refusing to pay more than six million dollars in taxes to the municipality, the mining companies left in excess of twenty million tons of tailings (an acidic toxic waste) behind, which has been connected to alarming cancer rates in the community.

Ron's friend, perhaps being aware of similar experiences, was struggling with balancing the importance of financial stability and the importance of the people and land that he loved. Ron guesses that this conflict contributed to a number of physical ailments that his friend began to struggle with, while also being deeply unhappy. Growing up he had been taught about respecting the earth and, in particular, being mindful of the places under the earth.

Ron remembers his friend reflecting on teachings he had received of the mīmīkwīsiwak, the little people who live in and care for the earth. Having love for his culture and for the land and wanting to make his family safe and comfortable were both extremely valuable, but the actions required in each were incompatible.

"Did the little people make him sick because he was helping the mining company take something that didn't belong to them?" Ron asks. "Maybe," he says. Ron also believes that his friend's physical illness and mental health struggles were exacerbated by the values conflict and that the stories and teachings his friend had received from his grandparents in childhood provided some much-needed direction in clarifying what mattered most. His friend eventually made the difficult decision to leave the job and take the risk of entering a completely different field, which Ron shares he became quite successful in and eventually retired.

Ron reflects on his own experience in choosing a career. Initially he had been interested in the criminal justice system and even spent some time working as a parole officer. But like his miner friend, he found this work in conflict with the kind of person he wanted to be and what he wanted to stand for in this life. He felt like the justice system was more focused on coercive management and revenue generation than on helping Indigenous people, and this is not what he wanted to be about.

NAVIGATING CONFLICTING VALUES AND TAKING ACTION

In our way of thinking, values are laws with the capacity to shape our lives. Yet as Ron's story shows, sometimes our values can come into conflict, pulling us in different directions. This tension between multiple things that matter to us can be a source of great distress, affecting us mentally, physically, emotionally, and spiritually.

You might find yourself torn between family obligations and personal growth, or between pursuing education away from home and staying to support your community. Perhaps you're grappling with the balance between forgiveness and seeking justice for past wrongs, or struggling to prioritize self-care while caring for others.

These conflicts are a natural part of our journey, but they can be challenging to navigate.

I am slowly learning that choosing a path in these moments rarely comes without discomfort or uncertainty. Acting in alignment with our values is never going to be clean or easy. It means making choices without guarantees, holding pain and love in the same hand, and sometimes letting go of what feels good in order to stay true to what matters. These teachings are clear in theory. The real test comes in the thick of crisis, grief, and loneliness, when the way forward is clouded and the only thing you can see is your own suffering.

GOALS, ACTIONS, VALUES, AND OUTCOMES

Ron spoke to how our values are a compilation of often unseen or underappreciated actions that end up being a vitally important part of a well-lived life. To illustrate this, Ron provides a teaching on the Sweat Lodge Ceremony.

"Many of us arrive at the Ceremony with the fire roaring and the Grandfather Stones already glowing red hot. We simply crawl into the lodge, and the Grandfathers are brought in and the Ceremony starts," Ron says. "But the Ceremony began much earlier." Three or four days prior to the Ceremony a conductor with the gift and abilities to conduct the Ceremony, along with their helpers (oshkapwewis), initiates preparations for the Ceremony. This may mean building the lodge, chopping wood, gathering medicines, and, most importantly, finding the Grandfathers, the stones that will be used to heat the lodge.

In each of these processes, Ron shares that there are specific protocols on how they are to be carried out in a respectful way.

Sometimes the things that we do in preparation for the Ceremony are hard. But each of these actions, even if they go unnoticed by others or appear to be a rather small thing in the grand scheme, are a vital part of the Ceremony.

We often believe that we have to engage in grand gestures to live a life of value. If I want to be a spiritual person, if I want to be connected to Creation, then I should complete a great pilgrimage, make a public commitment, and meditate several hours each day, right? Maybe. Each of those things could be really important parts of serving the values of spirituality and connection, but like chopping wood and collecting the Grandfathers, there are also many smaller daily actions that we do in preparation that are important, maybe even more important in the long run than any grand gesture.

This is where a lot of us get stuck. We think about what we must do to live a good life, and we identify huge life changes that must occur before we can be happy and fulfilled. To be happy I need to lose thirty pounds; then I will be more socially active and make new friends. When I finish school, I will feel confident in my work. Or when we are married, I will finally feel connected. Each of these statements reveal an underlying value, and perhaps some confusion about values, actions, and outcomes.

Values are our guiding principles, statements about how we want to be in this life, what we want to stand for, our Keewatin (North Star). Values cannot be accomplished and have no end. There will never be a point in my life where I can say, "There! I have achieved honesty," or "Finally, I have graduated from courage." These are things that we will have to continue to move towards until the day we die. If family and being a loving father is a value for me, I will have to continue moving towards that value for as long as I am alive. Even if I do the grandest gesture (taking the kids to Disneyland, rescuing them from a burning building, then buying them a sports car on their sixteenth birthday), I will still have to work at being a loving father.

Goals, on the other hand, can be accomplished. I could run a marathon, eat a healthy breakfast every day for three months, and drink eight glasses of water today. While each of these may be in the service of personal health (a value), I must still engage in the ongoing work. I cannot dust my hands off at a job well done and then sit on the couch destroying a bag of chips and a tub of ice cream from now on. Actions are all those little tasks that we engage in while working towards a goal. Goals and actions without values are impulsive, and values without goals or action are fantasy.

Outcomes are different still. Outcomes are not values or actions, but are the parts of ourselves and our world that are changed by our actions. Losing weight might be a consequence of the actions we take in the service of valuing personal health, but it's not the same as the value.

Why does any of this matter? Well, as in the first example (if I lose thirty pounds, then I'll be more active and meet new friends), there is clearly a value present (relationship and connection), but the actions are less clear, as is the connection between the anticipated outcome (losing thirty pounds) and the value.

This statement highlights a common pitfall that can keep us stuck. The value is unclear, there are few imminently achievable actions identified, and there is an overinvestment in outcome, which just sets us up to fail. While we might feel better about it, losing thirty pounds is not actually prerequisite to making new friends, and the focus on that outcome may be what has kept us away from real connections with others.

CARRYING OUR HEAVY BLESSINGS

When my values were tested in grief, these teachings became a compass, guiding me through the thick fog of loss. Inside that fog, everything familiar can feel strange. The landmarks that once gave shape to life, such as routines, relationships, and a sense of purpose, fade into the mist. It is easy to lose sight of what matters and to forget who you are beyond your loss.

Yet even in the darkest moments, values can serve as beacons, pointing towards a way of living that honours both the person you have lost and the person you are still becoming. Values are not goals to be achieved, but guiding principles to return to again and again. In grief, that compass becomes even more important. We do not "move on" or "get over it." We carry our loved ones with us, finding ways to live while holding them close.

There were times when I withdrew from others, not because I did not care, but because being with grief in front of people felt too vulnerable. We rarely talk about how awkward grief can be. Even with family and close friends, the exchanges often fall into a script: "I'm so sorry for your loss." "Condolences." "Thoughts and prayers." We say these things because we do not know what else to say. The mourner often ends up comforting the well-wisher, and both walk away feeling the gap between what was said and what was felt. It helps to meet this awkwardness with compassion, both for myself when I cannot face another interaction and for those who are trying, in their own way, to send warmth.

Every once in a while, I would hear something that landed differently. When a friend said, "May his memory be a blessing," I felt something. Those words did not try to patch over the hole or sidestep the pain. They simply acknowledged that my brother's life mattered, that he left ripples still moving in the world, and that it hurts because the connection was deep. They offered a reminder that the story of a life does not end with death and that grief can exist alongside gratitude.

In a nīhithaw worldview, death is not an ending but a transition. The spirit continues, and the relationship changes form but does not disappear. Our ancestors remain active presences in the life of the community. The teachings speak of the deceased as part of the land around us, the movement of rivers, and the growing plants. As everything is connected, a person's actions, intentions, and life force expand outward long after they are gone.

In our traditions, remembering and honouring the dead is an ongoing practice. We pick up their teachings, their stories, and their way of being in the world. We commit to having the experiences they did not get the chance to have and to finishing the work they began. It is a commitment to let their lives continue through us.

There are many ways to offer warmth to someone who is grieving without forcing words into the space. Sometimes silent presence is enough. Practical help, such as sending food (thanks, Lesley) or dog-sitting (thanks, John and Kendra), can ease a burden and allow them some space to be with their experience fully. If they want to talk, listen without trying to fix anything. Share memories if you have them. Acknowledge how hard it must be. Remember that grief does not expire; check in months later, not just in the first week. Create space for grief through memorials, feasts, or ceremonies if that is their way. Avoid phrases like "they are in a better place" that can close rather than open the conversation (since phrases like that are probably serving to allay our own discomfort with their grief rather than to really show up for them). Follow their lead. Let them set the pace and tone.

Many nations have practices that hold this understanding. Among Cree families, a sacred fire may burn for four days and nights after a death, a place for offerings and prayers. Annual feasts or memorials might be held for the first four years after someone's passing, sometimes longer. Vivian once told me that in the past, certain women in the community were designated cryers, invited to ceremonies to weep loudly for those who had passed. Their grief would encourage others to release what they had been holding in. The belief was that unexpressed grief could lead to illness, and that by making space for it together, people could let it come and go without becoming trapped by it.

These practices see grief as a shared responsibility, something expressed openly and shouldered together. They recognize that relationships with loved ones continue beyond death, shifting rather than ending. They also honour the teachings and stories left behind, treating them as gifts. Grief, in this view, is not a problem to solve, but a truly human experience that can connect us more fully to our communities, our ancestors, and the cycles of life itself.

KEEP ON KEEPING ON

As I pull away from the Linklater family camp, the dust from the gravel road swirling behind me, I find my thoughts being kicked up like the rocks that pound the wheel well of the rental. Ron's teaching that our values are inseparable from our kinship systems could probably inform a lifetime of study. It challenges the individualistic notion of values I have encountered in Western psychology. The teaching suggests that our values are not just personal preferences or abstract ideals. They are living connections that tie us to our relatives, including our other-than-human relatives.

When Ron spoke of love, respect, bravery, honesty, humility, truth, and wisdom, it was not in the context of self-improvement, but as guiding principles for how we relate to our entire community, human and nonhuman alike. What if our values are less about self-actualization, personal preference, or individual identity and more about finding our place in the web of relations? How would that change how I chose to act?

After the long drive I sit still and light my smudge, letting the sage curl through the air. The world feels still around me. My feet press into the floor, and I put my hand on the heaviness in my chest. My attention skips from my body to my heart, then to my mind, where thoughts of undone tasks, old memories, and unfinished conversations flit by. Beneath it all is spirit, that part of me that knows my place in the circle.

From that place, Ron's teachings feel less like abstract principles and more like threads in a living web. I can see where they were already woven into my life and where I need to strengthen the weave. Some of the next steps are simple, such as checking on someone I have been meaning to call or completing a task that will make someone else's day lighter. Others will take more courage, such as reaching out where there is distance or speaking words I have avoided.

As the landscape changes from prairie to forest, I wonder how this understanding of values might change our approach to healing and wellness in the Western world. If our values are tied to our kinship systems, perhaps healing is not only an individual journey, but also a collective one about the spaces and places we occupy and the roles we play in relation to those around us. Maybe living well is less about personal achievement and more about how well we weave ourselves into that ecological fabric of the universe Isaac had mentioned back at Nimkii. These thoughts and a fullness in my heart accompany me as I continue the drive east. The setting sun casts long shadows of birch trees across the road. I feel grateful for Ron's teachings, and I also feel the weight of responsibility that comes with them. I need to keep listening and learning.

13.

GLORIA OSHKABEWISENS-McGREGOR

Now our journey takes us to Whitefish River First Nation on Mnidoo Mnising, also called Manitoulin Island. It's a long and beautiful drive, and I can smell the life of the Great Lakes. I've always loved how it feels like you can fit more air in your lungs when you are near big water. The leaves are beginning to turn, and the black-and-white trunks of the birch trees stand in stunning contrast against the golden yellows, deep oranges, and fiery reds of their transforming leaves. Vast sheets of quartzite and limestone rise like old bones from under grass and moss. For billions of years, they've watched waters rise and fall and have experienced humanity like the blink of an eye.

Grandmother Gloria Oshkabewisens-McGregor greets me with a warm smile, her presence bringing a calm that immediately puts me at ease. Gloria is an Anishinaabemowin language teacher and traditional practitioner from Wiikwemkoong Unceded Territory who now calls Wiigwaaskingaa her home. As we settle into her cozy living room, I offer tobacco and tell her about the journey of learning that I have been on.

"Pain is something to be embraced," she says, "a valuable teacher." My ears sparkle at how her words join with the teachings I have already been given. "Pain isn't so much the problem as all of the words we use to talk about it," she adds. When speaking of anxiety, for example, Gloria likens the word itself to an alarm going off in a submarine in the deep. The brain attaches itself to the word and sends out a distress signal that is heard by the body. The heart seems to say, "Oh, we are panicking? All right, I will step up the beat down here." From there a sort of anxiety telephone game occurs across our body systems. Our airways feel constricted, our muscles tense, our stomach ties itself up in knots, and then the brain, sensing this bodily response, is quickly validated: "See? I am anxious."

I feel like Gloria is talking about me specifically, and I have the sudden sensation that she can see right through me. It is a bit unnerving, but also liberating, as if I can drop the heavy pretenses that we usually carry to block others out.

The words we use to describe our experiences are powerful enough to generate the experiences on their own. In the future, all we need to do is think of that word *anxiety* or any of its associates, and that familiar pattern of bodily activation and feedback to the brain kicks into action. Gloria points also to our urge to find a reason for our unpleasant experiences, and how difficult it can be for our minds when there is not a clear explanation. "Much of the time this is not possible, as the experiences may be the product of womb-space memories or blood memories from our ancestors," she says.

For a long time, science has dismissed teachings like "blood memory" as mystical or pseudoscience. Yet recent research on historical trauma and epigenetics has begun to explore how lived experience can leave biological marks that influence future generations. Some studies suggest that trauma may be associated with changes in DNA methylation, a process that can shape how genes are expressed, and some emerging evidence suggests that these changes may be observed across generations. Associations like these have been reported among Indigenous peoples in North America and in the descendants of Holocaust survivors. Still, the field of epigenetics is still in its infancy, and the findings with humans are mostly correlational at this point.

It's important to point out that First Nations teachings do not require scientific validation; they stand on their own. I'm not convinced that science will ever be able to capture the complexity of what Elders mean by blood memory anyway. There is also a danger in relying too heavily on genetic models of trauma that pull the focus further towards individual pathology and away from the current and historical social roots of intergenerational trauma. For me, it is enough right now to smile when I see science beginning to circle around something my granny knew when she was a little girl.

"By staying in the diagnosis of anxiety or using the word *anxiety* itself as an explanation for our unpleasant feelings," she says, "we are able to avoid both the discomfort of not knowing and the underlying causes that may be too painful for us to confront." But of course, this is where the vicious cycle of "difficult experience, move away, relief, and repeat" can begin.

Gloria does not believe that we are trapped in this loop, however. She offers a different perspective. "When we are afraid, the Elders will often say, 'Good, that shows you are human. Now walk through it!' Fear will never go away, so get to know it." Gloria says we have been trained by society to be led by our fear. Our brain screams, "Go, run, find the door," but our spirit has the capacity to listen to those thoughts and remind us that we are in our own bodies. Our spirit can be a parent to those thoughts and fears. Fear can challenge us in a good way, facilitate growth, and help us to re-evaluate our lives.

Gloria shares how fear invited her to grow during fasting ceremonies and when invited to share her story to a large crowd of people once. Moving through those fears required allowing her spirit to guide her. "Fear," she says, "tells us that we are standing at the edge of what matters." Gloria is careful to add that we should not ignore our fears and anxieties, as they may be telling us we are in real danger. After all, these difficult thoughts and feelings are working hard to protect us.

As our conversation deepens, Gloria speaks about what it means to live in a way that feels genuine. When I ask her about presence, she pauses and says that what comes to mind for her is the idea of being real. She explains that many of us have gradually drifted away from the truth of who we are, often without noticing it. Gloria describes the self as a single being made up of several interrelated places. She talks about the mental, emotional, physical, and spiritual as constantly influencing one another rather than operating in isolation. When the mental and emotional become caught in patterns of worry or conflict, the physical body often carries the burden of that tension. Over time, she says, this strain can show up in the body in very real ways. The spirit, however, relates differently.

Gloria explains that the spirit is not caught up in argument or defence. It comes from a place of deeper awareness, and its role is to experience this physical life and to help guide us through it. When the spirit is pushed into the background, our thoughts and fears tend to take over. When it is allowed to come forward, it can bring a sense of steadiness and direction. For Gloria, reconnecting with that spiritual place is central to living in a way that feels honest, grounded, and whole.

As Gloria sips her tea, I find myself considering each of these places within me, whether they are balanced or imbalanced, and what it is that I hope for in each place. Mentally, I want to nurture curiosity and keep learning in ways that connect me to others. Emotionally, I want to meet my feelings with honesty and compassion and to be present for the emotions of others without shutting down. Spiritually, I want to be my authentic self; I want to get better at seeing the world inside and out of me; I want to sit in Ceremony, spend time on the land, and connect with the spirits of others in a good and kind way. Physically, I want to care for my body by giving it movement, nourishment, and rest. Gloria shares that each of these domains can strengthen the others, but they all need our attention. Usually when we are struggling, there are one or more of these that haven't had our attention. I think a bit on how important this is when we are trying to find purpose and clarity in our lives.

Gloria also speaks of how fear and triggers can shape family life. She tells the story of a father on a healing path who becomes triggered by his child's tantrum. In that moment, he sees himself as a child again and begins to act like his own parent, repeating the cycle. Gloria explains that if the father can learn to take a single step back, even for just a second, and notice from a place of spirit, he can truly see his child as his child and not as the pain of his past. From there, he can choose to respond differently. He can offer what he himself once needed. In this way, fear becomes a doorway into clarity and healing. "Even this," Gloria says, "is a teachable moment." Awareness, even for the brief moment afforded by a deep breath, can create space for a choice aligned with love.

"The one you are missing is you." Gloria shares that the Anishinaabemowin word closest to what English speakers might think of as "me" or "I" is *niin*. She explains that this word does not function in the same way as the English *I*. It does not refer to an isolated individual. Instead, it asks you to consider others in your actions and decisions.

When someone says *giiy-niin*, meaning "no, not me," or *niin ga zhichige'we*, meaning "I will do that," the statement still carries a sense of responsibility to what is happening around them. The word itself reflects consideration. It suggests that a person has taken into account what has occurred, what is needed, and who else is involved. In this way, the English idea of a self-contained "me" does not quite fit.

Gloria explains that this way of understanding the self is tied to a broader teaching about unity. When we speak about ourselves as a people, she says, we often say *ngo dwe waangozme*, which is sometimes translated as "we are all one." This does not mean that everyone is the same, but that we all participate in life in similar ways. We breathe, we eat, we see, we walk, and we live here together, on this earth, in this moment.

She adds that this understanding shapes how we relate to one another and to ourselves. If the self is always formed in relationship, then care for oneself is never separate from care for others. Identity is not something that ends at the skin, but something that is continually shaped through connection. Gloria often returns to the idea that remembering this kind of relational self can bring us back into the present, grounding us in what is actually happening now rather than in stories of separation or isolation.

Gloria speaks often about how modern life trains us to function as instruments rather than as whole people. She uses the image of tools like hammers and screwdrivers to describe how society relies on us to keep things running, often without regard for our inner lives. Expectations built into systems such as rigid sick-leave policies or limited bereavement time, she explains, can require people to set aside grief, pain, and exhaustion in order to keep operating. Over time, Gloria warns, this kind of pressure teaches us to suppress our natural responses. Feelings that have no space to be expressed do not simply disappear. Instead, they are carried in the body, sometimes showing up later as physical illness or emotional distress. In her view, this is what happens when people lose touch with their own capacities for care, reflection, and self-guidance.

Gloria's teaching is a reminder of the importance of identifying and living by our own values rather than exclusively on societal expectations. Sometimes we need to say, "I won't be your tool today," and to reconnect with our inner selves, she says. This perspective challenges us to reflect on our own journeys and how easy it is to get caught up in external pressures, losing sight of what truly matters. Gloria's teachings encourage us to reclaim our autonomy, honour our emotions and natural processes, and resist becoming mere tools for societal function. Instead, she advocates for a more balanced approach that honours our interconnectedness while also respecting our individual needs and values.

Gloria also emphasizes the importance of retreating and spending time with oneself. As she puts it, "The one you are missing is you," a reminder that presence requires more than being physically surrounded by others. For Gloria, self-reflection is essential to clarifying values and restoring balance. She speaks about fasting ceremonies as one powerful way of creating that space. Time alone on the land, away from conversation and distraction, allows a person to sit with themselves and listen more carefully. In those moments, she explains, what has been pushed aside often begins to surface. As I listen to Gloria, I am reminded of similar teachings I've heard from other Elders about the necessity of solitude and reflection. I think about my own experiences of feeling overwhelmed and how easily I can lose sight of myself amid daily demands and responsibilities. From this perspective, reconnecting with the self becomes more than a psychological exercise. It becomes an act of calling one's spirit back.

At times, Gloria speaks about how difficult it can be to sit with oneself. When we slow down, she explains, the internal noise often grows louder. Thoughts and feelings that have been pushed aside begin to surface, and the impulse to distract ourselves can be strong. Her words resonate deeply, reminding me of moments when I have avoided being alone with my own inner world, choosing activity or busyness instead.

Gloria often returns to the paradox of loneliness. Many of us move through our lives feeling disconnected, even when we are surrounded by family, partners, children, or community. We can be in a room full of people and still feel utterly alone. From her perspective, this loneliness is not always about the absence of others, but about distance from oneself.

One of the most striking aspects of Gloria's teaching is her insistence on the sacredness of this self-connection. She speaks about retreat and seclusion not as avoidance, but as a necessary practice. Time alone can become Ceremony, a way of listening and remembering who we are beneath the roles and demands placed on us. Seen this way, moments of withdrawal can carry meaning and purpose. This understanding shifts how I think about experiential avoidance. It softens some of the judgments I have held about pulling away from things. Every choice to turn towards ourselves, even when it requires stepping back, can be an expression of what we value most. As Gloria once reminded me, "You need to take care of yourself because you are part of other people's lives."

Gloria's teachings challenge the isolated Western idea of the self. She shows us that the self necessarily carries the other within it. This view resonates with the science of psychological flexibility, which understands the self as dynamic, relational, and shaped through our social experience. Our community teaches us to observe and describe our own behaviour.

When we are children and we fall, our mom or auntie or granny would say, "Oh, you hurt yourself," or they might say, "You look so mad!" when we are having a tantrum about something. This and a multitude of similar interactions compile themselves into our self-image in our early life. And we only need help for a little while, because before long, we can use our big brains to make our own self-labels and self-stories, the "I am" stories we discussed earlier with Vivian and Isaac. This collection of stories, descriptions, and evaluations is what the science of psychological flexibility calls our conceptualized self or *self-as-content*.

Gloria expands this picture of self by insisting that a healthy self is not a collection of isolated traits but a being in relationship, shaped by responsibility and connection to family, community, and land. This points to another layer of self, what contextual behavioural science refers to as *self-as-context*. I once heard Dr. Russ Harris compare our thoughts and feelings to the changing weather and our true self to the unchanging blue sky. Gloria's teaching that "the one you are missing is you" also speaks to this. She points towards the self that remains present beneath our stories and judgments, the spirit that persists even as experience changes. It is easy to mistake what is happening within us for who we are.

"You already know how to reach." Gloria's teachings emphasize the sacredness of everyday actions. Even simple daily tasks can be approached as Ceremony, she says, and even if they are small, they can fill our lives with meaning and purpose. Every choice we make can be an expression of our values. But where do we start? And how do we live a values-based life in the face of so much pain and suffering?

I remember Gloria telling a story about walking along a road and losing your footing without realizing it. In her telling, the mind becomes so busy that you don't notice the ground changing beneath you until you suddenly find yourself down in a pit. Everything you were carrying in your head settles into your body at once, and even small movements begin to feel heavy.

She talks about how, from that place, the way out can look impossibly steep. When you're down there, perspective collapses, and what might actually be a manageable climb starts to feel like a solid wall. The longer you stay still, the more convinced you become that you can't move at all.

Like Len, Gloria shares that many people are never taught how to carry heavy loads of pain and experience. At the same time, she emphasizes that we already possess the basic capacities needed to move ourselves in a different direction.

"You know how to use your arms and legs," she says. "You know how to push and pull." Then she pauses and adds, "You're the one who has to reach."

The first movement is rarely confident. It often feels strained and uncertain. Still, once that small effort happens, something begins to change. The ground doesn't look quite the same, and the next step becomes imaginable.

As Gloria finishes, I sit with the image of myself looking up from a set of muddy tire tracks. I think about the times I've felt buried under the weight of my own thoughts, the times I've mistaken standing still for action, or surviving for living. So many times I've slipped into depressed inaction by staring at that wall. But a small reach, a breath, a step forward is almost always possible, and with enough of these, the way ahead slowly comes into view.

I hit the road away from Gloria's place feeling her words in my bones. She has reminded me to walk through fear, to find the sacred in self-connection, and to see that even the small gestures and actions within each day can be Ceremony. On the ferry south across Georgian Bay, I stand at the window looking as the *Chi-Cheemaun* ("*Big Canoe*") cuts its path through the water. The sky is wide and pale, with little Bob Ross fluffy clouds floating above my head.

As the wake stretches behind, back to the island, I think about how easy it is to lose sight of myself in the rush of daily life, especially in the face of pain, grief, and self-doubt. Maybe the one I have been missing is me. Maybe I have been holding grief, difficult thoughts, memories, uncomfortable sensations, and self-judgments so close that my spirit could not see much beyond them. What would it be like to hold them a little lower, closer to my heart, so that I could see the wide world out there?

So, we can't ever be rid of difficult thoughts or memories. As Dr. Steven Hayes has said, "There is no delete button in the human experience." What we can do, though, is pause, notice, and reach. A small gesture that slows the spin of the mind, makes space for our spirit, and turns us back towards what matters. Each breath, each choice to notice, keeps us on the road. Out on the water, I feel the invitation to reach. To let fear and grief come along, but not let them block the horizon. To come back to myself.

GOOD ACTION AS A WAY OF BEING

Mitho-tōtamowin, acting good, means recognizing and embracing what we stand for, identifying our core values, and committing to actions that reflect those values. In this active way of being, we clarify the sources of our life's meaning and pursue increasingly effective actions guided by these principles. When our goals and actions align with our values, we engage in a life of purpose and fulfillment. Values and committed action are essential ingredients in the recipe for a meaningful life.

Values are the compass points that guide us through the wilderness of human experience. They're the qualities of action that light us up inside, that make us feel like we're living, truly living. Values are directions we choose to move towards rather than destinations we arrive at. You can cross off goals from a list or reach a final achievement. Values are more like the North Star, always there, always guiding, yet never fully reached. Being a loving parent, for instance, is an ongoing journey, a direction you keep choosing, day after day, diaper after diaper, teenage door slams and eye rolls and all.

Committed action is where the rubber meets the road. It's where we start taking steps, sometimes baby steps, sometimes giant leaps, in the direction of our values, even when our mind is screaming bloody murder about all the reasons we can't, shouldn't, or won't succeed. This requires doing what matters, when it's easy and especially when it's hard. Committed action often involves discomfort and a willingness to experience discomfort. This means making room for the inevitable anxieties, doubts, and fears that show up when we step outside our comfort zones. It's saying, "Hey, Anxiety, I see you there. Thanks for trying to keep me safe. You can come along for the ride if you like."

We can live a good life with meaning and purpose, even while we are feeling scared, uncertain, or downright miserable. Because at the end of the day, it's what we do with those feelings that counts.

It starts with figuring out what really matters to you, beyond the noise of societal expectations and your mind's constant chatter, and then taking steps in that direction, again and again, come hell or high water. It's challenging, as anything worth doing usually is.

TWO PATHS IN A YELLOW WOOD?

As we explore this concept of engagement, I'm reminded of a story that Dr. Matthieu Villatte once told me that illustrates the dance between our values, actions, and outcomes. It's a story that might feel familiar to many of us who've faced unexpected challenges while trying to connect with loved ones. Picture this:

A recently divorced father who shares custody with his ex-wife wants to make the time he spends with his two sons count. He recalls being out on the land with his own dad and one time when they hiked up a trail in a local conservation area and spent the afternoon in a great spot overlooking the valley. He decides that this coming weekend, he will take his boys out there and share some stories about his own father, who has long since passed.

They get to the conservation area and start to head in the direction of the lookout. As they get close to the trail entrance, he sees it is fenced off and marked with a black and yellow DANGER: DO NOT ENTER sign. A passerby tells them that the trail is closed, as they are doing some work after some significant erosion has made parts of the path unsafe. The father is disappointed and apologizes to his sons while swearing under his breath. It begins to rain, and he realizes that he hasn't packed any rain gear. He is completely deflated, feels like a failure, and spends the remainder of the day sulking before dropping his sons off at their mother's house.

Or . . .

Upon discovering the closed trail, the father takes a deep breath and asks himself what is most important at this moment: connecting with his sons and honouring his father's memory. He turns to the boys with a smile and says, "Looks like we need a new plan. What do you guys think we should do?" One son suggests exploring a different trail, while the other proposes building a shelter. The father, embracing flexibility, agrees to try both ideas.

As they walk towards the other trail, he begins sharing stories about their grandfather, pointing out plants and wildlife his dad taught him to identify. When it starts to rain, the father sees an opportunity. "You know, some of my best memories with Grandpa were camping out in the rain." They gather some fallen branches, and the father teaches his sons how to make a simple lean-to, just as his father taught him. They talk about what they might eat if they were stranded out there. This sparks a creative conversation filled with laughter.

As they walk back to the car, soaked but smiling, the father realizes that while the day didn't go as planned, he succeeded in spending quality time with his sons, sharing his father's wisdom, and creating new memories. He doesn't feel a sense of accomplishment because of any specific outcome, but because he stayed true to his values even in the face of unexpected challenges.

Both versions of the father's experience show us something important about living our values. In the first scenario, we see how easy it is to get caught up in our plans, to let unexpected obstacles throw us off course due to overinvestment in outcome. But in the second, we witness the power of values clarity, of staying connected to what matters most even when things don't go as we hoped.

This story is about a father and his sons. And it's about the choices we make when life doesn't cooperate with our plans. How do we honour our values and take action when the path ahead looks different than we may have expected or wanted?

What might change in our own lives if we approached unexpected obstacles with this kind of flexibility? How might we deepen our connections, honour our values, and live more fully if we could loosen our grip on specific outcomes and instead focus on that North Star?

The beauty of living this way is that even when the outcomes are not what we hoped for, we can still take heart in knowing we acted in line with our values. This alignment itself is a form of success, one that nourishes our spirit and strengthens our resolve for future challenges. The good life doesn't demand perfect outcomes. It just requires us to keep walking in the direction of those things that are most important in our lives.

As I think about Ron's and Gloria's teachings and the ways values and actions weave together, I find myself returning to a question that has followed me through my own grief and through sitting with the grief of others: What kind of father, partner, sibling, son, friend, human being do I want to be during this difficult time? Years from now, how will I want to remember the way I acted?

In my own losses, the answers to those questions have often been simple, though not easy. I have wanted to be present with my family. I have wanted to honour my loved one's memory. I have wanted to face each day with as much grace as I could manage.

It was never about doing those things without fear or sadness. There were days I felt guilty for moving forward, days I was exhausted or convinced I should be doing more. I learned that the feelings could come with me. I could still make the call with a lump in my throat, still take the walk with heaviness in my chest.

Living our values through grief is not about achieving perfect composure or making grand gestures. It is about showing up in the ways that matter most to us, even when it is the hardest thing we have ever done.

14.

BUT IT STILL HURTS

Carrying our heart through grief does not mean we do not feel pain. The pain is still there, and some days it is overwhelming. In the weeks and months after Jerome died, I found myself dodging calls, cancelling plans, and building walls. The grief was so heavy I couldn't stand to see it out in the world. Somehow the experience of grief is worse in front of other people. There are certainly times when our thoughts, memories, emotions, and physical experiences can be completely overwhelming. At these times, maybe the best we can do is turn towards our heart and keep walking? Let me explain . . .

While I was training to be a psychotherapist, Lesley and I had the privilege of being supervised by Benjamin Schoendorff. He's a brilliant psychologist and an expert in clinical applications of RFT. I was working with my first few clients in therapy and was starting to find my voice, to learn to build relationships and trust with people who were struggling with their experiences.

I once asked, "Benj, what do we do when you're sitting with someone and they completely break down, like full crisis mode, hyperventilation, hysterical crying, dissociating, right in front of you just having a really bad time?" There are a ton of strategies for moments like this: box breathing, the 5-4-3-2-1 grounding exercise, feet-press grounding, orienting by gently saying their name, offering a cold glass of water, using a textured object for tactile grounding, progressive muscle relaxation, self-hugging, butterfly tapping, dropping anchor, paced breathing, etc. I wanted to know which was best, what exactly I should do in a situation like this. Benj paused for a moment and put both of his hands on his head, which he usually does before something brilliant comes out.

"Well, what kind of helper would you like to be in that moment?" He looked at me and waited, his chin now resting on his fist.

"Umm . . . a supportive one, I guess?" I wasn't expecting a question to my question.

"What does that mean?" he said, nonplussed.

"I suppose I would like to be empathetic, patient, safe, and present." Another long pause.

"Well, there you go."

I did not like this answer, and I'm sure he could see my cognitive floundering.

"Look," he said at last, his hands returning to the top of his head, "there are of course tons of techniques you could try, many things you could say." I was hoping he might at least list the top five. "And each and every one of those techniques could blow up in your face."

As usual, he's right. I've heard of people having panic attacks when prompted to engage in deep breathing, and I've certainly had the experience of a "validating reflection" just pissing a person off more. I recall, for example, being called a terrorist and receiving a loud open-hand slap in the face in response to a poorly delivered "I can see how frustrated you are right now" early in my career.

"Sometimes the only right thing to do is to turn towards the kind of helper you want to be in that moment—empathetic, patient, safe, present, whatever—and be there with the person and their pain." Damn that's good, I think to myself. "And then whatever you say or do, at the very least you can look back and know that you did it in the service of those values." I doubt Benjamin even remembers dropping this absolute gem, but it has become a sort of internal mantra in my helping work and in my own healing.

* * *

By orienting to our values and taking small action, brick by brick, we create a life that is rich and meaningful, even in the midst of loss. When we lean towards the kind of partner, parent, son, daughter, or friend we want to be, towards what we want our lives to be about, we can walk with fear, anger, sorrow, or joy with an open confidence. When we lean towards the kind of relative we want to be for the ones we've lost and the kind of relative they would have wanted to be if they could be here with us now, we are able to continue our relationship with them in a new way. By living our values and theirs, we can hold on to the best parts of what we shared with them.

Jerome was a quiet guy, and people may have assumed that this meant he did not have much going on upstairs. But the opposite was true. He held an incredible amount of knowledge about history, politics, and philosophy. He was a voracious reader. I had seen him finish full-length books in a day, only to have another in his hand the next morning. He had a kind of savant talent for trivia and crosswords, even calling out correct answers before the contestants on *Jeopardy!*, which was always good for a laugh. When I take action to learn new things, to read, or to engage with material outside my comfort zone, I like to think I am channelling Jerome's value of curiosity.

In the end, maybe grieving well is about choosing a life of vitality, even when that choice hurts. We grieve well when we create a life that our loved ones would be proud of, a life that honours their memory by living fully. I often ask myself, "What can I do today to practise truth, wisdom, humility, and courage?" and "What can I do today to honour those who have travelled on?" The things that work are usually small and manageable.

This path is not easy. But as we continue to choose a life aligned with our values, we may find that we are not just surviving our loss, but growing through it. And in doing so, we find that our pain, while still present, becomes more than just pain. It becomes a testament to the love we shared, a force that propels us forward into a life of meaning and purpose.

Again and again, I have returned to the teachings that Len, Isaac, Renée, Ron, and Gloria shared about pain as a teacher and a blessing. I will admit that my mind fought these teachings at first. How could there be anything in this loss that could teach me? How could this stabbing in my chest ever be a blessing?

About a month before he passed, I sent Jerome a T-shirt that said, "You'll Always Be My Brother, Vato Loco" (a reference from the movie *Blood In Blood Out* for the uncultured heathens out there who may not be familiar with this cinematic masterpiece). He sent me a picture of him wearing it with a big smile. About a week later, I must have dialed his number without realizing it and hung up. He called me that night, which was unusual since he would normally send a text or an email. I answered, and we went back and forth, exchanging the usual "How have you been" and "What's up" and had a good chat. After about ten minutes, I think we were both waiting for the reason for the call to surface. Eventually, he asked, "Did you call before?" I checked my phone and saw that I had. We both laughed and promised to see each other soon. I did not realize that would be the last time we would speak.

Sometimes that memory is painful and sometimes it makes me smile. I am grateful for that strange twist of fate. I never thought I would be so happy to have butt-dialed someone.

That accidental call, that last conversation with Jerome, has stayed with me. At first, the memory was almost too painful to bear. The "what-ifs" and "if-onlys" crowded my mind, threatening to drown me in regret. Over time, I began to see it differently. That random call gave us one last chance to connect, to laugh together, to say, "Take it easy, bro," without realizing it would be the last time. That feels like a blessing now.

It has made me think more about the little moments we often overlook. The casual conversations, the inside jokes, the shared silences. Grief has a way of making these moments shine like precious gems in our memory. Now I try to be more present in my interactions with loved ones, more aware of the potential preciousness of each exchange. The pain of loss has heightened my appreciation for the life I am living and the connections I have.

This awareness, this presence, this appreciation of here and now, is how pain becomes a great teacher. Grief has taught me to cherish the present, to value each interaction, each shared laugh or tear. It has shown me strengths I did not know I possessed.

Nothing opens your heart to the pain of others like having your own heart broken. As a helper, I have become more attuned to the struggles of those around me, more willing to sit with them in their discomfort without trying to fix it. Grief has expanded my capacity for empathy, making me a better listener, a better friend, a better human. And grief has inspired me to try to embody the best of my brother, to give the difficult parts to Creator, to let his best qualities live on through me, to do the things he may have wanted to do but never got the chance to. Now that I carry him with me, I believe that I am a better person. So yes, in addition to being extremely painful, even grief can be a blessing. The pain is not gone. It never will be, and I don't want it to be.

CULTURE AS MEDICINE

Cultural practices all over the world offer time-tested ways to clarify our values. Whenever I come upon some difficulty, a conflict with a colleague or a difficult decision, my mom will often ask, "Did you put your tobacco out?" Usually the answer is no, as I always get so caught up in my own head that I forget to pause and ask the universe for some help. Then when I am out by the water or under a tall tree, holding the tobacco in my hand and reflecting, I at least get at what is actually important and what is just noise.

Having tea with an Elder or an older person also offers an excellent opportunity for values clarification. Dorothy Elie, a great-grandmother and Elder from Batchawana, always makes me laugh when she says, "There's Elders, and there's just regular old people." Whether they are Elders or not, our relatives who've been on the earth through many decades often carry insights from long lives of hardship, love, loss, and joy, and they tend to have great stories. Engaging with storytelling as both a listener and a storyteller allows us to explore the meanings behind our experiences.

Engaging with our languages offers a pathway to a more fulsome clarity of our values. Learning, reclaiming, or practising Indigenous languages is an active form of survivance. Each phrase, each word, and each morpheme contains layers of meaning that are infused with the values of our ancestors. The fact that the word *heart* is found within the word for "tongue" and for "truth" is a powerful example of this.

If you know a language keeper or are able to take classes or learn in some other way, investigate the words that represent those things that are most important to you. Find out how the words are constructed and what their meaning is. Language shapes how we think, how we understand ourselves and our place in the world. When we engage with our ancestral languages, we're engaging with worldviews that have sustained our people through countless generations.

THE GRANDFATHER I BECOME

I open my eyes to big drops of water splashing off the top of my head. Remnants from an overnight thunderstorm, if my nose serves me right. I guess I've fallen asleep in a wooden chair under a tarp that has seen better days. Everything is blurry. I fumble for the glasses sitting on my head, tied to a bright-orange string so they won't fall off, it seems. Once I slip them on, the world sharpens. A stone firepit sits in front of me. It's a familiar fire that I have sat beside over many years. To my left is the little blue cabin that could use a new coat of paint. Clothes sway on the line, and somewhere close by, children laugh.

I look at my hands and startle. I am so old. My palms are etched with deep creases and cracked like dry earth. My knuckles are rough and weathered with thick calluses like my father's. I touch my face and feel the folds, the heavy bags under my eyes, the big ears, the thin white braid hanging down my back. My body aches in every joint when I try to sit straighter. I sink back into the handmade rocking chair, its pine grain darkened with burn marks, fitted perfectly to my shape. On my feet are beaded slippers, each with a bear surrounded by tiny stars.

From around the corner, a little one bursts into view, calling out: "Nimosōm! Nimosōm!" Her long black hair streams behind her, her brown skin glowing, her eyes the green-grey I know as my own bloodline. She climbs into my lap and squeezes me tight. The hug hurts my bones but fills me with warmth.

"Who's your mom?" I ask, my voice low and gravelly.

She looks at me as if I've forgotten myself. "Mommy!" she says, perplexed.

"Yes, of course. Mommy." I nod.

Her eyes cloud with worry. "Nimosōm, I feel so scared." I stroke her cheek with my cracked hand. "What is it, cāpān?"

"I don't know. Maybe somebody's mad at me. Maybe I did something bad. My heart feels like it's trying to jump out of my throat." She presses both hands to her chest, her breath shallow.

I see it all in her face—doubt, fear of being left behind, fear of not being enough. Tears gather. I hold her, then gently set her back so I can look her in the eye.

"Everything you feel is trying to teach you something," I tell her. "Even the ones that twist your stomach and pound in your chest. They don't feel good, but they are helpers too. They try to protect us, even when they make us miserable. I fought with those feelings for many years—kicked and cursed at them. It never worked. Hard feelings belong here, just as much as laughter and play, just as much as tears and worry. They are part of being human."

She listens, her eyes wide. I poke her belly with my finger, and she giggles. "The real you is here," I say. "Your spirit. I knew your spirit before you were born, and when I go to the spirit world, I will still know it. It is a good spirit, kind and pure. The feelings and the stories your mind tells are only things you have. They are not who you are. So when they come, be gentle with them. Thank them for trying to do their job. And remember that your spirit is the one who chooses, the one who connects, the one who knows what matters."

I look down at my wrinkled hands resting in my lap. "Someday soon I will go to the spirit world. When I go, I'll leave this body and its worries behind. I'll cross that rainbow bridge with only my spirit, and those I love will be waiting. One day, when you are old and wrinkled like me, I will come for you. Then we will go fishing."

Her face breaks into a wide smile.

"I love you, cāpān," I say.

"I love you too, cāpān," she answers before running off towards the cabin.

What if we could give that same kindness, compassion, empathy, and understanding that our great-grandparent might give us, or that we might give to our great-grandchildren, to ourselves? It is often easier to imagine offering a gentle, compassionate response to someone else than it is to extend it inward. Yet we carry the same voices, the same strength, and the same resilience within us. When we are uncertain, we can return to this place in our minds. We can ask together, WWMCD? "What would my cāpān do?" And we can listen for the answer.

BRINGING IT HOME

After visiting with Ron and Gloria, I am even more convinced that the teachings I've gathered resonate with the core principles of psychological flexibility while adding a rich cultural and spiritual context that science often seems to leave behind. Mitho-tōtamowin, as I've come to understand it, involves knowing what we stand for in life and then taking action aligned with those values. Dreaming big isn't enough; we must also live out our values in tangible ways, and usually in the presence of discomfort or challenge.

The Seven Grandfathers—wisdom, love, respect, bravery, honesty, humility, and truth—provide a powerful framework for identifying and articulating our values in a way that taps into a shared ethos that prioritizes collective well-being over individual preference. When Ron speaks about mino bimaadiziwin coming from Creator, he's emphasizing that living according to these values is a sacred and shared responsibility rather than a matter of personal preference.

Gloria's teachings on the nature of the self as being inseparable from consideration of others further highlight the interconnected nature of our values and the committed actions they suggest. Her emphasis on the four aspects within us—mental, emotional, physical, and spiritual—reminds us that true engagement involves our whole being, not just our thoughts or behaviours.

Both Ron and Gloria underscore the importance of community in our journey towards engagement. This may be a point where Indigenous helping wisdom and psychology diverge. Value clarification, as conceptualized by psychology, is often positioned as an individualistic process. It is about the individual discovering what matters most to them in the absence of external influence. In fact, a common practice in many therapies is to try to determine sources of external influence on values and discourage them. Of course, this might make perfect sense if someone is engaged in some behaviour that is completely meaningless to them or causing them harm, just to please another person (e.g., pursuing a career that makes you miserable to keep your parents happy).

Locating meaning in the desires of the collective and in what most benefits community, even when this involves sacrifice, distress, or discomfort, enhances our understanding of living a good life. Ron's story about his cāpān beautifully illustrates how our values are inseparable from our kinship systems, and how value systems extend across generations. This also ties into the concept of committed action—our choices don't just affect us, but ripple out to impact our families, communities, and even future generations.

UNPACKING

After every trip there's that moment when you get home and set your bags down in the doorway. You hug your partner or kids or dog or the pillow you missed so dearly, and for just a moment your home feels new and strange. But then you breathe in the air, turn the lights on, and your body remembers that you belong here. You pull out the gifts people sent back with you, bannock wrapped in a tea towel or some weird knick-knacks you found on the road home. My mom would always come home with that multicoloured popcorn from the airport. I can't think of a better feeling as a kid than the mom-popcorn combo.

Some things go into the fridge, some end up sitting on the kitchen table for too long, but eventually they get washed, folded, and put back where they belong. The teachings we gather need time to find their place too.

So here I am, back at my desk with a cold cup of coffee at 2:30 a.m., trying to figure out what the hell to do with everything I've collected. My notebook is full of chicken scratch, my computer has too many folders and files with names like cyh_v6_final_final_ACTUALLY_final.doc. So before trying to tell you what I think it all means, as if there could be one neat answer, it feels important to pause and look at what's actually here. To sort through it and to pause at the place between one journey's end and the start of the next.

That's where we are now.

CARRY YOUR HEART, LIVE A GOOD LIFE

I found this good life. I found this sense of well-being. As we move from one teaching and ceremony to the next, we become stronger and more capable in how we conduct ourselves in relationship with our spirit, our Mother Earth, our family, and our nation. It all comes together and helps us live as strong, good people. A'ho!

Ron Linklater

15.

THE GOOD LIFE

So what does it mean to live a good life? We human beings have been asking this question at all four corners of the earth for a very long time. At our core, we yearn for safety, meaning, and belonging, and we put much effort into fulfilling those yearnings from the time we are born to the time we travel on. It isn't just that these things bring us comfort. We also know that their inverses—danger, confusion, and isolation—can do us great harm. So as we cultivate and collect the things that we believe comprise the good life, we also seek shelter from needless suffering.

But does a good life mean an existence free from pain? Is a good life one without grief, sorrow, fear, doubt, anger, and loneliness? Does this require us to build an impenetrable tolerance for the troubles of existence or a transcendent state of mind untouched by material things? Does it require sacrifice, benevolence, recognition, wealth, or power? What does it mean about our relationships with others, with those whom we love, those who are unlike us, and with those who would do us harm? And most important of all, how do we get there? How do we live a good life?

Since time beyond memory, we have worked hard to answer these "good life" questions, and we have come up with just about as many answers and theories as there have ever been people. Indeed, defining the good life and generating a set of instructions to obtain it have been the key preoccupation of philosophers, healers, educators, governments, and religious institutions since their inception.

Perhaps because we are all working with a similar set of perceptual tools through which we view our world, there are many points of convergence in the explanations and recommendations we have developed for one another. Whether it be philosophy, psychology, medicine, law, or religion, most of our cultural systems attempt to provide us with some understanding of human nature, on the origin, topographies, processes, and functions of our experiences, be they cognitive, emotional, behavioural, physiological, or spiritual. They all seek answers to the existential questions that haunt us: the purpose of life, the nature of knowledge, the boundaries of our free will and mortality, and the meaning of reality and our own existence. They all have some interest in human potential, in how we can be safe, be well, and flourish as individuals, as families, and as communities.

Our cultural institutions are also usually concerned with the nature of suffering in one way or another, on remedies for physical ailments, methods of caring for emotional and spiritual wounds, how to obtain peace and safety, and how to find relief from the many forms of suffering our bodies, minds, and spirits endure. In a way, it makes sense that there would be many points of convergence in the philosophical, psychosocial, and spiritual systems found around the world.

In spite of these points of convergence, however, there are just as many points of divergence in the maps we have made on the path to the good life. Of course, this should also be expected to be the case given the heterogeneity of our contexts. As human beings, we may be gifted with similar tools with which to interact with our worlds and similar questions, but we certainly have different ancestors, live on different landscapes, speak different languages, have experienced different histories, and tell different stories. Surely these contextual differences influence our perspectives on suffering and what it means to be well.

We need only look to the thousands of distinct religions and specialized areas of psychotherapy to see the diversity of opinions on the "what" and "how" of our good life question. Unfortunately, these points of divergence are not without consequence. Rather, they have been the cause of most of the atrocities we have committed against one another and against our nonhuman relatives during our short time on this planet. So while much work has been accomplished, the route to the good life doesn't appear to have got much clearer with the passage of time, and it seems we are moving quickly towards a point of no return in our ongoing assault on one another and on Mother Earth.

I must confess one last time, I have unfortunately not found the solution to human suffering or the answer to our good life question. Instead, what this journey of listening and reflecting has shown me is how little I actually know, and how much more I still have to learn and experience.

A while back I was working after midnight, on my fourth coffee, yelling at my computer, which was acting up while I was trying to complete a self-care workshop for First Nations helpers, and seeing me in this state, Lisa said, "Are you sure you're the one who should be teaching people about self-care?"

We had a good laugh about that. It was the reminder I needed in that moment to go easy on myself and to be a human being. That is the spirit, the shared humanity, and the humility I hope these pages have conveyed. I haven't reached the summit of my personal healing and learning mountain; far from it. In offering my experiences, I share only from my own steep path upwards, one that sometimes has good, solid footing and other times has unexpected ice patches and loose stones. But from here, I can look across the valley to where you are climbing your own mountain, and I can share what I can see with the hope it might illuminate something useful for your journey. And in reciprocity, the perspective from your journey will hold insights that can, in turn, teach me. We are fellow travellers now, after all.

The idea of trying to define the good life within the pages of a book seems a bit silly. I can hear my great-grandmother boom with laughter at the idea of me trying to find the good life within the pages of a bunch of books rather than by a warm fire out on a smooth rock at the edge of the lake or at a kitchen table, teasing and being teased by my relatives. But good words can be medicine, and I believe it is important that we capture as much of the knowledge from our Elders as we can for the generations that will follow, so I'll give it a try.

Miyo-pimātisiwin is a comprehensive worldview that integrates emotional, mental, spiritual, and physical aspects of life to promote overall well-being. It is rooted in Cree and many other cultures; it emphasizes the critical importance of living harmoniously within one's community and environment. The concept fosters self-determination and cultural identity by maintaining a delicate balance among the different realms of existence—human, other-than-human, natural, and spiritual.

At its core, miyo-pimātisiwin is a way of sustaining good relationships with all elements of life. It encourages collective contributions and support systems that enhance emotional and mental wellness through shared resources, prayer, storytelling, and the healing power of family. These practices strengthen communal bonds and ensure that cultural values and traditional knowledge are preserved and passed on. It empowers both individuals and communities to resist and thrive. It nurtures a way of living that is intertwined with our ancestors, linked to our descendants and all of Creation. It reminds us that well-being is contingent on connection.

I like my friend Dee's answer better. Dr. Dolores (Dee) Subia BigFoot is a marvellous human being whom I have had the privilege of learning from and being in Ceremony with. While studying at Harvard, I got to visit with Dee's ancestors and be a very small part of her work on repatriating the remains and belongings of the ancestors of many nations from museums to their rightful homes. She is a tiny Grandmother, but she is massively powerful. I am confident she will be successful in this important work. She once told me a story about an experience she had in southern Alaska.

As a world-renowned child-trauma psychologist and expert, Dee was asked to evaluate the state of family wellness in a certain community along the southern coast. She visited there and sat with children, families, and Elders in circle. She asked, "What does wellness mean to you?" as she was eager to centre the community's perspectives and needs in this project. An old granny stood up and proclaimed, "Smoked salmon!" As Dee is a member of the Caddo Nation of Oklahoma and has had little exposure to fish camps for the salmon harvest, she was understandably confused by this at first.

The Elder went on to explain that at the fish camps, when the community came together for the salmon harvest, they experienced a wholistic form of wellness that embodied all aspects of a good life. The physical act of harvesting and preparing salmon provided exercise and nourishment, addressing bodily health. Emotionally, the camp fostered well-being through the joy of visiting with family, sharing stories, and laughing together. Mental wellness was promoted through problem-solving, settling conflicts, and engaging in the cognitive challenges of traditional practices. The spiritual dimension was nurtured by giving gratitude for the land's bounty and participating in Ceremony. Socially, the camp strengthened communal bonds across generations, from Elders to newborns. It reinforced cultural wellness through exposure to language, traditional teachings, and practices passed down through generations. The direct interaction with the land and its resources fostered environmental wellness and a deep connection to nature.

In essence, the fish camp represented a microcosm of miyo-pimātisiwin, where every aspect of wholistic wellness was addressed in a single, culturally significant practice. It demonstrated how traditional activities could simultaneously nurture physical, emotional, mental, spiritual, social, cultural, and environmental well-being, all while ensuring the continuity of knowledge and practices across generations. This simple answer of "smoked salmon" encapsulated the complex nature of wellness, and I think did a much better job than my academically oriented brain could ever come up with. Be like smoked salmon, my friend.

KITA-PIMŌTĀTAMĀN KITĒH

Kita-pimōtātamān kitēh. This teaching given to me by my gifted relative Ken Bighetty translates from Cree to something close to "I walk while carrying my heart"; although it is true that an English translation can never really capture the meaning of a phrase like this accurately. At its essence, I believe the teaching means that all of the parts of us are meant to be held with care rather than set aside, even when they are cold, heavy, or sharp. The good life, or miyo-pimātisiwin, comes from this way of walking.

To carry our heart is to turn towards our experiences with willingness and compassion. Gloria taught me that to fear is to be human. When we walk through that fear with care, we honour the spirit that has worked so hard to protect us our whole lives.

Isaac often spoke about pain as something meaningful rather

than something to be eliminated. As he put it, "Our pain is useful." Pain, he explained, can teach us where our boundaries are, how we are affected, and what we need in order to stay whole. In that sense, pain invites reflection, growth, and careful listening to what our spirit, heart, and body are asking of us.

Len spoke about willingness in a similar way. He described how allowing ourselves to feel what is present can bring us back into alignment. When we stay with our experience, rather than turning away from it, we remain connected to the moment we are actually living. From that place, he said, we are better able to process what we are moving through and continue forward in a good way. Carrying our heart in this sense becomes an act of reconciliation with ourselves. Even small gestures of self-love, forgiveness, and compassion can gently turn us back towards our own hearts.

* * *

To carry our heart is to be present. Our spirit lives in the now. Presence is a way of inhabiting life fully. It is the cold wind on our face, the tension in our chest, the story in someone's eyes, the butterflies in our stomach, and the rock in our shoe. It is how we bring our full attention to the person across from us and to the land beneath us. This way of walking invites us to see from a place of spirit. It opens us to the wider web we are part of. Isaac said that the good life is attached logically to the plants, to the animals, to the sun, to the stars. Vivian reminded us that when one is suffering, all are suffering; we share our grief and pain. Carrying our hearts in a good way means carrying the hearts of others as well. This is reverence and reciprocity at work.

To carry our heart is to bring our values into the daily movements of our lives. Cooking for loved ones, caring for our homes, tucking our children in at night, and tending to each other are all offerings. Each gesture becomes Ceremony. Preparing a meal embodies hospitality and gratitude. Cleaning our homes prepares space for spirit, for story, and for care. Offering a ride to a relative or volunteering at a youth program strengthens our families and communities. For those living far from home territories, carrying the heart can take creative forms. It may be learning the basics of language in an online class, smudging in a small apartment, or joining a beading or drum circle. Of course, Ceremony offers an action-oriented path to healing and connection that can't be replaced. Whether it is a fast, a sweat, a morning smudge, or a shared song, Ceremony gives form to our values. When we gather together in circle or in celebration, we create a space where our individual stories weave into that collective fabric.

To carry our heart is to learn. We seek teachings and we pass them on, extending the thread of connection. Over time, the thread stretches across generations and wraps around nations and the world. Carrying our heart means teaching as well, sharing in a manner that allows people to grow, stumble, and rise again. We live the good life when we share with the young and the old, with those who are curious, and with those seeking wellness and belonging. Every small act of teaching strengthens the circle and shapes a world that will be worthy of the children who will one day learn to carry their hearts here.

To carry our heart is also to help. Extending care to others brings medicine into our own lives. Each gesture of kindness creates a line between hearts, a circulation of spirit that restores balance for both the giver and the receiver. Helping strengthens our own spirit because the energy we offer also nourishes us. Walking with others in their struggles teaches us endurance and deepens compassion. Sharing food, guidance, or listening strengthens our place in the circle of care. Helping reminds us that healing comes from relationship, and every offering of support ties us more firmly into the fabric of life. Carrying the heart in this way makes helping and healing a single, continuous path.

To carry our heart is to move through life with an emotional willingness, a spiritual attention to ourselves and the universe around us, and a commitment to use our minds, words, and bodies in a good way. We carry our heart when we hold our responsibilities, joy, grief, fears, and longings in a way that we would want our descendants in the many generations that will follow when we are gone to sing songs about. But living the good life is not a performance. It is a practice. Learning to walk and to be happens both within the moments when we are forced to be our truest selves and also in the everyday simple and mundane movements of our lives. We must walk it each day through effort, reflection, and relationship. We stumble and take detours and return to it when we are ready. We carry our heart through the quiet days, the joyful ones, and the ones that ache. So if you walk with experiences the world has labelled anxiety, depression, grief, or trauma, know that you never walk alone. Remember, in the end it's you and the tree, and absolutely everything and everyone else.

As this part of our journey together winds to a close, the questions we began with echo still: How do we live a good life and carry our hearts with us along the way? The knowledge, stories, and reflections shared here offer no final destination, only supplies for your path towards miyo-pimātisiwin. The wisdom gifted by the Elders and Knowledge Keepers we met form the heartwood of our time together. Their words carry a familiar truth that somehow dances with insights also found within the science of psychological flexibility. Bringing together the great helping philosophies of our world creates possibility, and there are many more to explore.

I believe that we may find something really great at the place where Indigenous helping knowledges and the science of psychological flexibility intersect. I also believe that the field of psychological science can be enhanced by Indigenous helping knowledges in ways that improve its relevance and its ability to take on the increasingly complex problems in our world. The teachings shared by Len, Renée, Isaac, Vivian, Ron, and Gloria have a depth and relational sophistication that extend far beyond any psychological technique. They offer relationship where there has been distance, spirit where there has been abstraction, and context where there has been generalization. As Dr. Hayes reflected, the science is arriving where our knowledge traditions have been all along. There, now I've said it three times.

If any part of this book has moved you, I invite you to reflect on the responsibilities the teachings carry. Rather than content, perhaps you can treat them as gifts rooted in relationship and moved from one heart to another. I think the best way to honour what you've read is to seek your own relationships, with teachers, with land, with language, and most of all with your own story. I hope you will hold these teachings with humility and care; I promise to do my best to do the same.

THIS IS NOT THE END

For weeks, I struggled with how to end this book. An ending feels like goodbye, and there is no word for "goodbye" in Cree. An ending also feels like I have concluded my learning and healing journey, which of course I have not. So instead of an ending I'll complete the circle and return to where we began.

Early this morning, as the sun began to rise over the tree line,

I drove out to the bridge where, more than twenty years ago, I had once sat on the edge when my heart had turned its face away from me. I set my present-day hands on the cold steel rail and look down at the rocks below. Like me, the water flowing below has travelled far to get here.

North of the city, some high ridge carved by retreating glaciers thousands of years ago collects rain and snow, its porous soils and gravels filter all impurities as gravity pulls it down into massive underground aquifers. In the darkness, the water crawls over clay and shale towards lower ground. Where slopes and valleys cut into the earth, the pressure builds like a tilted sponge, spilling the water out into daylight. Springs, ponds, and wetlands form first trickling streams and then rushing tributaries before meeting powerful river currents on their way towards kīhci-sākahikan, the great lake.

On my journey from that broken young man with his feet dangling over this bridge in the middle of the night to the helper, partner, and father I am trying to become, I have crawled through darkness too. I know now that in these sinking moments I was being purified. That the journey through dirt and gravel was a blessing.

I open my left hand and drop the tobacco I have been holding and watch as the wind takes it swirling down towards the water. By the time this book is published, it will have been four years since my brother began his journey. In Cree protocol, we feast his spirit each year, and on the four-year feast we acknowledge his completed journey to the spirit world. It is a celebration and a release, a recognition that he has taken his place among our ancestors.

Whenever any of us six boys were acting too macho for our own good, flexing in the mirror or puffing out our chests at one another, my mom would always say something like "Mahti, awas! My granny walked five miles back and forth from her trapline every day carrying all her gear on her back well into her eighties. She could wrestle you to the ground with one arm! You better watch it; she'll be waiting for you in heaven!"

While I can smile at the thought of Jerome wrestling various freakishly strong grannies in the spirit world, I know that my heart will always feel a sinking heaviness at the absence of his physical presence, that thoughts of guilt and regret will always whisper in my ear, and that my mind will always time-travel in a DeLorean fuelled by "what-ifs" and "if-onlys." But I also know that each of these are a mirror image of the continued presence of his spirit, the gratitude at the moments we shared, and the life I will live in his honour. That the things my mind has labelled pain are also love. I will carry both as a precious gift until I can set them down and start my own journey.

This journey of gathering words, revisiting old blessings and sorrows, and wrestling complex teachings from their context onto the page has itself been a humbling experience in learning to carry my own heart. On several occasions I've had to fight the urge to chuck my computer (and this book) into the river. Yet the words that were shared with me shone like a glowing North Star, reminding me that there is something here that is important to share.

I hope you carry something from our time together. Our pain can reveal our greatest teachings. Our spirit finds home in the present moment and in the identification of the self as part of, rather than separate from. Our full engagement with life, in all its beauty and challenge, brings us meaning, purpose, and belonging. Each day, let's work to find the strength to be present, the compassion to embrace it all with open arms, and the courage to carry our hearts gently on our way to the good life.

Ekosi.

ACKNOWLEDGEMENTS

From the outside, writing a book may look like a solitary act, but in truth, it is the product of a whole community holding that pen together. I've had the privilege of learning from and being supported by so many great human beings.

First and foremost, I offer my deepest gratitude to the Elders and Knowledge Keepers who welcomed me into their homes, lodges, and hearts. To Grandmother Renée Thomas-Hill, Len Pierre, Isaac Murdoch, Vivian Recollet, Ron Linklater, and Gloria Oshkabewisens-McGregor: this book belongs to you as much as it does to me. Your generosity, humour, and wisdom are the true heart of these pages. I also owe a special debt to my friend and brilliant language teacher Simon Bird from Southend Reindeer Lake for all of his help on getting the Cree language right.

I am incredibly grateful to the team at Simon & Schuster Canada for believing in this project. A special thank-you to my senior editor, katherena vermette. You have been a guiding light throughout this strange and wonderful journey, and I am so thankful to have had the opportunity to learn from you. I also want to extend my gratitude to Nicole Winstanley, Chloe Gandy, and Emelia Gauch for all the ways you have helped bring this book into the world. Thank you to Paul Barker and Alan Jones for your design work, and a heartfelt thank-you to Tsista Kennedy for the incredible artwork that graces the cover; your vision captured the spirit of this work beautifully. To my literary agent, Cody Caetano at CookeMcDermid, thank you for your advocacy, your guidance, and for helping me navigate this new terrain.

I have learned from so many great clinicians over the years, good people with good hearts, and I cannot possibly list them all here. But I must mention Lesley Barreira, Benjamin Schoendorff, Tera Beaulieu, Dr. Dolores "Dee" Subia BigFoot, and Dr. Joseph P. Gone. And of course, Dr. Steven C. Hayes, for the incredible generosity in sharing your knowledge and expecting nothing in return, I am eternally grateful. I also owe a debt of gratitude to my own therapists, Dr. Lee Unger and John Jacobs. Thank you for always holding space for me, for your skilled guidance, and for helping me learn to examine my own experiences with kindness; it's not easy being a therapist's therapist!

To my parents, Lennard and Pauline Busch, you were my first teachers and my first examples of what it means to be a helper. Thank you for showing me the path. To my siblings, thank you for the laughter, the lessons, and the shared history. And to my brother Jerome, though you journeyed on before this book was finished, your spirit is woven into every page. Thank you for teaching me how love endures. To my partner and soulmate, Lisa Orsi, thank you for your patience and support during the long nights of writing, my noisy clacking away on too many old typewriters; you are the firm foundation upon which this good life grows. To my children, Sophia and Felix, you are my reason to keep striving for that good life; you make me proud every single day. I hope this book serves as a wayfinder for you, should you ever need it. Finally, to my ceremony family, my ancestors, and Nisichawayasihk Cree Nation, I hope I have made you proud.

* * *

kahkithaw niwāhkōmākanitik kinanāskomitināwāw

* * *

All my relations. I thank you all.